WOMEN OF RESISTANCE
POEMS FOR A NEW FEMINISM

EDITED BY
DANIELLE BARNHART
&
IRIS MAHAN

O/R

OR BOOKS
NEW YORK • LONDON

For my daughters, Skyla Emerson and Cassidy Rilke—
and for my mother, Jacqueline. – D.B.

For my mother and my sister, and for the women who braved this
world before us, brave it beside us, and who will brave it after. – I.M.

Anthology selection © 2018 Danielle Barnhart and Iris Mahan

All rights information: rights@orbooks.com
Visit our website at www.orbooks.com

First printing 2018.

Library of Congress Cataloging-in-Publication Data:
A catalog record for this book is available from the Library of Congress.

British Library Cataloging in Publication Data:
A catalog record for this book is available from the British Library.

Typeset by Pauline Neuwirth

Published for the book trade by OR Books in partnership with Counterpoint Press.
Distributed to the trade by Publishers Group West.

paperback ISBN 978-1-944869-79-3 • ebook ISBN 978-1-944869-80-9

10 9 8 7 6

CONTENTS

SECTION II

SECTION III

SECTION IV

INTRODUCTION

> I am, she said,
>
> though borne into demolition.
>
> —*"Poem for Suheir Hammad" by Trish Salah*

This anthology does not have a singular purpose. It is part love letter, part manifesto, part confession, part wish—and those are just the raw materials.

It is also a meditation on grief. We grieve for the women we have lost, the violence and oppression we endure, and the children who will never make it to the terrifying and glorious world of womanhood. These poems surge forward with defiance and insist on the power and endurance of the feminine spirit. The work here breathes, occupies space, and demands attention, not only for women, but for all who fall into the category of other within the bright white patriarchy.

We exist through acts of demolition—as one would walk through flames, and come out on the other side. This book began as the idea to engage in a small act of resistance. In the aftermath of the 2016 election, you could find us commiserating on barstools in the Village, sniffling through a poetry reading, or consoling one another during late night phone calls. We found ourselves pondering that historic act of resistance, that fight for agency through suffrage. As poets, we wanted—*needed*—to know what suffrage meant to other poets.

Here we required a definition, but also a history. The word "suffrage" in its Latin form *suffragium*—meaning "support, ballot, vote"—did not come into such popular usage in English-speaking nations until the U.S. began drafting its Constitution in the 1770s. *Suffrage* came from Middle English, meaning *intercessory prayer*, or prayer on behalf of others. What power does a vote hold when cast for an oppressor? What do liberty and freedom really mean when they are empty words that were exclusionary then, and remain so? The Suffrage Movement was a galvanizing success and a heartbreaking failure, and it is in this place of strength and brokenness that we began the work of this anthology. We shed the suffrage, and began with an invocation on behalf of otherness. "What can we do?" one of us would ask. "You are doing all you can—you are enough," the other would reply. "You are alive."

We are, but it continues. Powerlessness, poverty, assault, unjust legislation, mutilation, degradation, rape, forced sterilization, and murder have all been used as means of controlling women and shaping our realities, for countless generations. Whether large portions of the population have chosen to ignore this (or continue to ignore this) does not change it. And yet for many, there is a growing sense of urgency that simply wasn't there before. Whether due to privilege, willed ignorance, lack of information, or caprice, many of us have been able to shield ourselves from the truth. But the truth is that we are all in danger, and we are all suffering. Some of these dangers are glaringly obvious, others more insidious, but all are real, and incessant.

Equally real, incessant, and varied are our passions, our strengths, and our stories of triumph. This is how we found our way to creating this anthology. While there might be some universal truths, there is no universal experience. Attempting to speak for one another, or for women as a group is unacceptable, and often destructive. For too long women have canceled each other out—silenced other individuals in favor of a supposed unifying movement—and it has been a travesty.

In her essay, "Women and Honor: Some Notes on Lying," Adrienne Rich writes:

> Women have been driven mad, "gaslighted," for centuries by the refutation of our experience and our instincts in a culture which validates only

male experience. The truth of our bodies and our minds has been mystified to us. We therefore have a primary obligation to each other: not to undermine each other's sense of reality for the sake of expediency; not to gaslight each other.

Women have often felt insane when cleaving to the truth of our experience. Our future depends on the sanity of each of us, and we have a profound stake, beyond the personal, in the project of describing our reality as candidly and fully as we can to each other…

When a woman tells the truth, she is creating the possibility for more truth around her.

This book is a collection of truths. These poems are personal truths of intersecting feminist realities that make meaning not only from the necessary and varied individual experience, but from the context of their togetherness. May we all find ourselves in the moment of listening closely, and in knowing that we have been heard.

— DANIELLE BARNHART AND IRIS MAHAN

EDITORS' NOTE

This resistance affirms that *womanhood* is not limited to the biology of the female body, although this resistance supports the intuitions that protect those (both biological and identified) bodies. This resistance proudly supports Planned Parenthood and the Center for Reproductive Rights, which protects the choices those bodies can make. This resistance does so by giving portions of the proceeds of this collection to these protectors so that they may go on protecting.

Above all, this resistance exalts those bodies—the bodies of women, of femmes, girls, and all gender-nonconforming people. The bodies of this collection are touched against their will, bombed, stoned, they are giving birth, they are bending and not breaking, they are crying, they are shouting, they are raging. Beyond luck, they thrive. From ashes rising, from rubble resounding, these bodies are borne and forged indestructible by the fires of demolition.

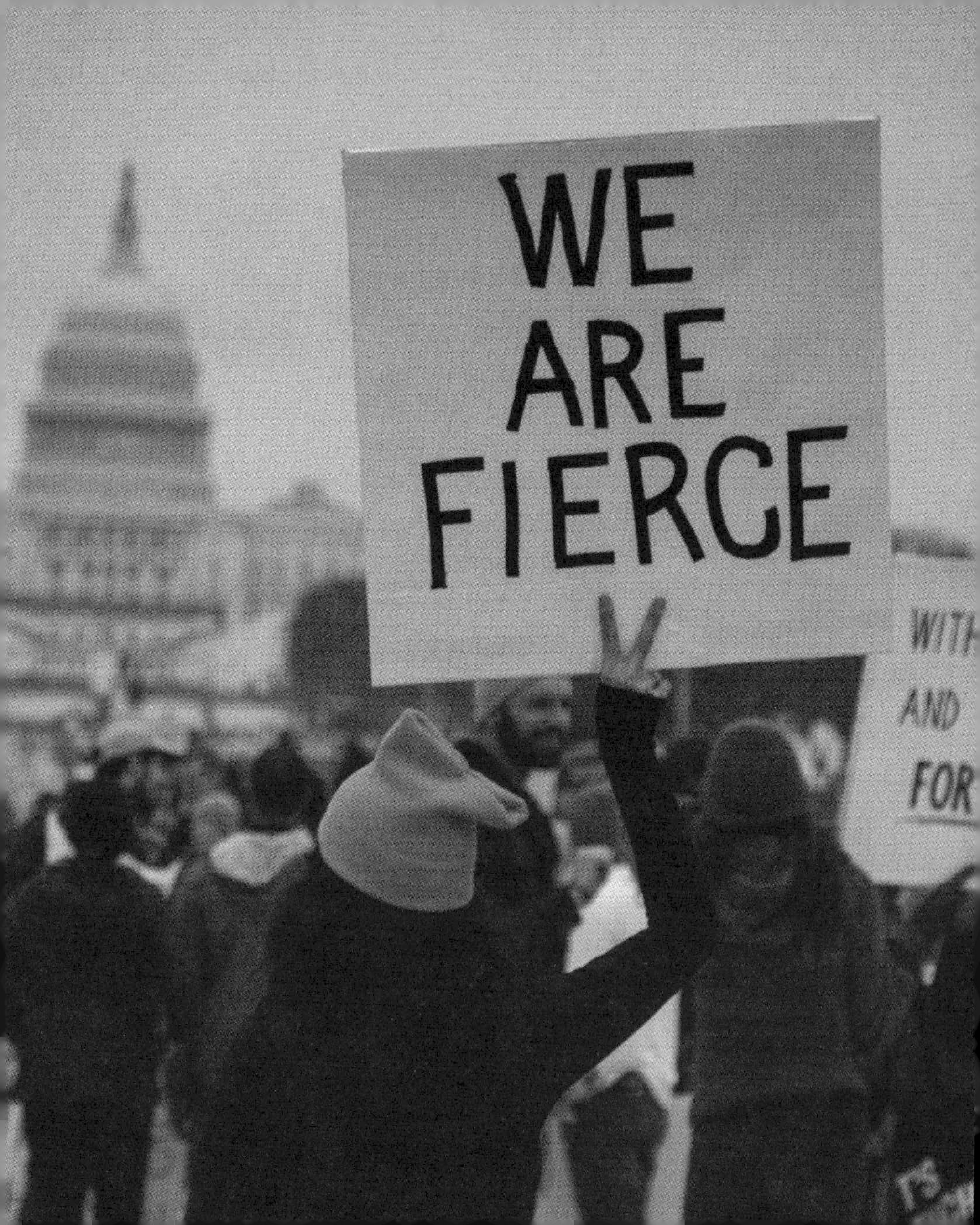
WE
ARE
FIERCE

SECTION I

DENICE FROHMAN

"A WOMAN'S PLACE"

i heard a woman becomes herself
the first time she speaks
without permission

then, every word out of her mouth
a riot

say, *beautiful*
& point to the map of your body
say, *brave*
& wear your skin like a gown or a suit
say, *hero*
& cast yourself in the lead role

///

when a girl pronounces her own name
there is glory

when a woman tells her own story
she lives forever

all the women i know are perennials—
marigolds, daffodils
soft things that refuse to die

i don't come from anything tamed or willing
i come from soil flossed with barbed wire

meaning, abuela would cuss you out
with the same breath   she kissed

you with   her blood
a wild river

my mother   doesn't rely on instruction manuals
or men   nor does she equate the two

can fix anything
if you get out of her way

says the best technology
is her own two hands

///

but once, i dreamed   i had no teeth
just a mouth   to hold
other people's   things

if this poem is the only thing that survives
me

tell them i grew a new tongue
tell them i built me a throne

tell them when we discovered life on another planet
it was a woman
& she built a bridge, not a border

got god & named *gravity*
after herself.

DENICE FROHMAN

HUNGER

a woman can go mad
without herself, you know
can call a lover
(who convinces her
there is sweeter fruit
than her own name)
a lover
and never
sleep good again.

I want to believe
I'm a better woman now
that I'm writing poems.

that when I say, *poems*
I mean another way
to say, *revenge*.

that when I say, *revenge*
I mean to regift each shard of god
back to its maker.

that when I say, *god*
I mean to grow fat off my own honey
and never go hungry again.

LAURA FAIRGRIEVE

BAMBERG, 1628

"The witch appears to have alternated between being a terrifying enemy who could bring ruin and death and a pathetic figure to be despised and insulted."

—Robin Briggs

Each forget is a whisper of hot water brushing chapped skin
These fingers are branches sewn together from different trees
As the men slow danced with fallen cornstalks
I chewed dandelions that hadn't grown beards yet
For hours shadows licked at my ears
Swallowed my eyes down their tunnel throats
The winds were whipping dust into fog
I saw a bed thrown through a window
It was sanded into smoke tripping over the trees
The night had turned the air to fire
The hot earth grabbed my ankles until it touched bone.

SALLY RIDE SPEAKS TO THE SCHOOLGIRLS

Don't believe the quiet heat that waits to pull
your velocipede to pieces
when you pedal like you're tired of waiting.
Someone will want to solder your throat shut
while your mind turns figure-eights around
faceless people who promise you
space travel is one hundred years away.
Do not close your mouth for them.
Speed comes to anti-gravity paint
the hacked up remains
of spoiled shoe laces and band-aids
that stew on the blacktops, awaiting no rescue.
Run fast enough to crack your scabs,
run fast enough to hear
your arteries turn all your thoughts to nothing
more than a righteous racket.
When I flew to the edge I was neither sight nor
sound, not a grayscale photo
I was speed
I was the hand that holds the storybook illustration
I airbrushed the shadows clean off the page

I was an acrobat courting the cold-blooded stars
I was the slingshot that pulls itself impossibly taut,
that kisses its spine good-bye.
I counted backwards and my bones became hollow
I steered a shuttle with no space for pins or needles
sometimes chasing weightlessness is the only way
to keep your blood blitzing, to remember the
years you spent writing out equations,
whispering promises to cramped book spines,
answering barbed questions, remembering
you're the first
and sitting up straighter.
I raced against the rest with
no sir, not a single tear shed
Danny Dunn turned anti-gravity cartwheels in my dreams
and there was no divide
my interstellar medium, X-ray visions and Canadarm arm
shot me straight up
I did not wait for outerspace to extend its arm to me,
I thrust my face skyward
where no tinted glass could have spared me
where a breathless canvas of black beckoned me close
where I offered my ear, I reached out my matte limbed machine
and snatched a shuttle whole
where the sun would have happily frozen me to death
if I drifted too close.

FEMALE

Locker-room truant in a locked stall

Through study hall

Hiding, hand-stifling her cries,

A girl wide-eyes the unimagined smear

Of blood rusting

Her fingertips. Secret, quaint horror.

Some betrayal of the flesh has left her

Vulnerable,

Her blithe pellmell

Redefining to this singularity. But no.

She is smarter

Than her body. She will starve

This woman out, she will run and outrun

The turncoat moon.

She will firesale down

To a shoestring inventory: item:

Two eyes, indifferent

Blue; item: brain and brainstem;

Item: one mouth, tightened like a screwcap

On the business end

Of the pipebomb she's just become.

THE CHILDREN'S CHORUS

I want to sing in the Children's Chorus at the church because it looks like so much fun. I am confirmed when I am seven, because I can read the Bible and discuss what I have read. I am allowed to join the Children's Chorus because I can follow the lyrics in the hymnal. The pastor speaks to my mother after church and offers to pick me up and take me home so I can make all the rehearsals. I am the youngest member of the chorus. The pastor says I'm pretty. The pastor calls me into his office. The pastor lifts me up and puts me on his lap. The pastor kisses me. I squirm, tell him I don't like it, don't like the line of waxed hair above his lip. The pastor grabs my kicking legs, my thrashing arms. There is a gap in my memory here. I am grateful. There is a kaleidoscope of blackness, with those tiny, white floaters that come when I squeeze my closed eyes shut and hold my breath. I am grateful. When I tell my mother what happened, she is silent, then tells me, in a tiny voice, that I don't have to be in the Children's Chorus if I don't want to go.

CIVIL RIGHTS

When I think about the Civil Rights Movement, I think about the pastor. He is a prominent voice of the people, a man who is doing truly great things for our community. He fights for the rights of children to study in integrated schools and has been arrested multiple times so that little boys and girls, like me, can do the best they can in this life. How old am I when I am taught the lesson that my female body must be a sacrifice for the greater good? I am seven years old when I am taught to be silent, that no one will believe me because he is a handsome, powerful, charismatic clergyman interviewed on the nightly news and I am a quiet, studious, black girl with pigtails, cheap anklets slipping into the heels of my patent leather Mary Janes, with one beautiful parent in my home, passed out, drunk on the couch. And if they believe me, then what do I want? I have to know what I want, have to have the answers to the questions that are sure to come next. What did I do wrong? I feel like a soldier coming home from a war she never signed on to fight. For years, I wake up screaming from the same recurring dream: A man in silhouette sings, "We Shall Overcome," and locks all the doors in the world to touch me here and here and here—and still, they claim he is our revered leader.

THE RIDE HOME

I am walking down Franklin Avenue. There is a little neighborhood bar on the corner of Crown or Carroll Street, one of those almost-home streets. I remember hugging the curb when I get in front of the bar, always hugging the curb, never wanting to get too close to the dark glass or the insides. But this day, somebody calls out my name and I turn around. It is a man who used to come over and visit my mother sometimes. He works as a security guard in our apartment building and he is always nice to my mother; he is always nice to me. He asks me if I want a ride home; he says he is going my way. I think it is crazy that he wants to drive me home such a short distance...but there I am in the front seat and he locks the doors. I am in the front seat and he pulls up my skirt. I am in the sixth grade and I am smart but not smart enough not to get in the car with a man who has been in our living room and laughed with my mother. *Don't you remember the pastor? Don't you remember anything at all?* I am nine years old and in the sixth grade and he pulls up my skirt and says if I tell I'll just get him in trouble and no one will believe me anyway and he moves his hand beneath my skirt and this is all I remember of it, I swear. *Give us the date. Give us the time. What was he wearing? Did you tell him to stop?* Oh, yes: I remember the sky screaming; the sky that day was so incredibly blue. I remember telling my friend down the hall and the two of us, together, telling my mother. I remember that the next time I see him, he has two broken legs with pins in his knees. He says he will always have those pins in his knees to allow him the freedom to bend his legs. He says the cast, the pins, the metal...he says that all of this is all my fault, for telling on him and not keeping our secret.

NAOMI SHIHAB NYE

NOT EVEN

Did you hear her this morning, Yemen crying?

Weeping for arched windows

crushed for nothing

and the people who dwelled therein,

to whom can she wail?

Syria, sobbing for years now, Palmyra, Aleppo,

the ghosts of gracious avenues,

Syria tilts an ear, but cannot save herself, much less Yemen.

Or Palestine, gasping to the south. So tired. So very tired.

They'd help each other if they could but they cannot.

Don't ask a man to help. Don't ask any man.

Smudgy-faced child behind rubble, no more mother,

who remembers a better life?

What you think your own fear and worry, just a scrap of

sorrowing wind sweeping worldwide—

it's not new.

It's not even you.

JAMES ALLEN HALL

IMAGE

Catherine Opie,
Self-Portrait/Cutting,
dye coupler print, 40 x 30 in. (1993).

The model turns her back to us, hair shorn to the nape,
tribal tattoo circling her tricep, which, when flexed,
is a warrior's, but now hangs limp as a spear, unpoisoned.
She is naked. Maybe our looking unclothes her, searing

the image on her back: a house, scratched red into her flesh,
just beginning a lifetime's scab. Two windows, a door.
Two open eyes and a shut mouth and all the poisoned words
are in their beds, looking out to the front garden,

where two girls in red skirts hold hands among the tulips.
But the model can't see them. I tell her she can drop the knife,
but there's a bruise the size of a fist at the base of her neck.
I tell her the girls are in love, if love means *drawn in blood*,

the scar of your childhood will never heal.

JERICHO BROWN

OF THE SWAN

The luck of it: an ordinary body
Soothed once

Under God. No night ends his
Care, how

He finishes a fixed field, how he
Hollows

A low tunnel. He released me
After. Why

Else would I pray like a woman
Who's ruined

A man's ever-bitter extremity?
Men die,

But God's soul rises out of its black
Noose, finds

Bared skin a landscape prepared
For use

Where worship makes for immortality,
And I am

The Lord's opening, a woman
On earth

With pluck, with sting, with feathers
Left round my hide.

THE LEGEND OF *BIG* AND *FINE*

Long ago, we used two words for the worth of a house, a car,
A woman—all the same to men who claimed them: things
To be entered, each to experience wear and tear with time,

But greater than the love for these was the strong little grin
One man offered another saying, *You lucky. You got you a big,
Fine* _____. Hard to imagine—so many men waiting

On each other to be recognized, every crooked tooth in our
Naming mouths ready like the syllables of a very short
Sentence, so many of us crying *mine*, like infants who grab

For what must be beautiful since someone else saw it.

THIS IS WHY WE ARE AFRAID:

In late fall, the neighbor has an abundance of doe to process. He must be an impeccable shot. He must fatten his family all winter on what he collects from those early Saturday mornings in nearby forests. Sometimes there are so many that he must work the whole night to get through them all before the rot sets in. He walks in circles on his back porch, slicing through and shaving down with his well-sharpened tools until the animals' solid shapes have been whittled into a pile of precise and well-stacked steaks. The prominent veins of his forearms swell beneath his rolled up sleeves, and his cheeks puff and color. His blueness rises to his skin's surface from the exertion. On these nights, he brings out the work lamps best suited for his task. Their light is that particular hue—blue, and so very cold. In their blinding and icy brightness, his form looks more hulking than usual. He takes up so much of the scene that we can almost forget what is hidden behind the movements of his large, quick hands. If not for the hoof hanging from the overhead hook. If not for the distinct sound of a lengthy rip. Of something soft being torn open.

This is why we are afraid:

The thing about it is, once interior parts of us are brought outward, there is no way to put them back inside. At least not completely. Their wetness slicks across surfaces, soaks in. No matter how thorough the cleanup, there is always a thin layer that remains. This is what happens when blood leaves a body. A deal is made, and our blood now belongs to the pavement, to the upholstery, to the cold porcelain lip of the bathtub. Even years later, after countless sponges and solutions have passed over the area, a special liquid can be poured there and will glow blue with confirmation of what once spilled out. The original blue colors we see running beneath our pale skin can be restored well after they turned red, then rusted, then washed away. We are trying to tell you that we can never be fully erased. There will always be small drops of us waiting to be noticed. We do worry that this will somehow make him angrier.

This is why we are afraid:

There are too many shades of blue. Some are subtle—the pale aqua of shattered glass. A translucent trace of it only noticeable in small, fractured pieces. Only when looked at from above and slightly beside. Like the glass holds secret waters. Like maybe we all have unknown colorations waiting to reveal themselves until after we are broken apart. Some are more insistent—the stain of berries and rhubarb on the white cotton shirt we shouldn't have been wearing. The conspicuous blue. The blue of morning. The blue of mourning. The blue of mooring. The blue that is a darkness made visible.

This is why we are afraid:

The starlings that live in our backyards are arrogant with their flitting. They twirl and dive and scatter their iridescence with the confidence of young women, of powdered faces, of short hemlines brushing across strong thighs. They don't seem to know how soft their bones are beneath that pomp and plumage. How a (careless) person might not see them resting in overgrown summer grasses. How the weight of a distracted foot could cause their whole skeleton to collapse into itself. How a (ruthless) person might stalk and catch them for the sole purpose of feeling their skulls crush beneath the power of his hands. The quiet pop that precedes a conclusion. How their bones are soft blue as eggshells. How they are fragile containers at the whim and mercy of a flicking wrist. Their roundness so smooth and perfect it deserves a pronounced crack across its face.

TO THE WOMAN CRYING UNCONTROLLABLY IN THE NEXT STALL

If you ever woke in your dress at 4am ever
closed your legs to someone you loved opened
them for someone you didn't moved against
a pillow in the dark stood miserably on a beach
seaweed clinging to your ankles paid
good money for a bad haircut backed away
from a mirror that wanted to kill you bled
into the back seat for lack of a tampon
if you swam across a river under rain sang
using a dildo for a microphone stayed up
to watch the moon eat the sun entire
ripped out the stitches in your heart
because why not if you think nothing &
no one can / listen I love you joy is coming

JUDITH BAUMEL

SNOW-DAY

What was it drove me to insist on sleds,
to pull the children out of the playground
and toward the park's much steeper hills, instead
of making angels? I was waist deep and bound
by ice, and they were too. In their eyelashes
was unremovable ice. They crawled and flailed
on snow. The progress of their grudging limbs
slow. Surely memory of snow-fort caches,
the childish city happily derailed,
its hopes of milk and bread and papers dim.

When I was young I came to Boston late
late late one winter night from Baltimore.
The pre-dawn, post-blizzard of seventy-eight
glowed in the silent town where dump trucks bore
their loads of snow as through a secret city—
filling and then dumping in the harbor,
filling yet again. I'd just removed
a child from my womb. Well someone else did it
and it was not a child but some small scar
inside. It meant nothing to me, that newt,

that early fetus, and the procedure meant
nothing except perhaps the end of fear
and queasiness. Today how I resent
the way sadness and loss are souvenirs
we're forced to carry with us. Listen—Happy
is the way I felt, and still I feel,
when I can shovel through the euphemisms
of those who speak for me. More happy. Happy
that forever will that speck, that organism
remain forever small and unfulfilled

in contrast to my son who came exactly
ten years after to the day, and to
a woman ready for him. I had wept
returning to my now-lost lover anew,
seeing the streets of Boston being cleaned,
scraped clear of the invading snow
that clung to arteries, that fairly smothered
our chance to try to make a normal flow
of life. That struggle with the midnight gleam:
the wiping, tidying gesture of a mother.

GETTING A UTI

I went to the doctor for a UTI and I said to the receptionist "I have a UTI" and then I said to the nurse "I have a UTI" and then I said to the second nurse "I have a UTI" and then I said to the third nurse a male nurse "I have a UTI" and he said "OK we'll need a urine sample here pee into this cup" and when he looked into my urine with a microscope he said "you have a UTI" and wrote me a prescription

before the male nurse had come into the room the first time I said to the first female nurse "I don't want to be left alone with a male nurse or doctor" and she said "oh no we don't do that" and laughed and then I said to the second nurse "I don't want to be left alone with a male nurse or doctor" and she said "like just in general?" and I said "yes in general" and she said "oh ok"

when the male nurse came in the first time the second female nurse stood in the corner with her hands clasped together in a way I would describe as "nervously" it seemed like this was something she wasn't used to doing standing in the room with the male nurse and the patient

the second female nurse had just examined my kidneys for damage by having me lie down and pressing firmly on my back and side to check for pain or discomfort when the male nurse came in he said "I'm going to feel your organs for damage" and then karate chopped my back and abdomen pretty hard while I was sitting it was actually alarming it was hard to gauge whether there was pain in my organs or not because he was karate chopping so hard when I showed my boyfriend later how hard on his leg he said "ow"

while the doctor was karate chopping me I was thinking maybe he's mad because I asked to have a woman stand in the room and he's taking it out on me by karate chopping me but maybe he karate chops all his patients I don't know

LAURA THEOBALD

UNTITLED

i have forgotten what it feels like
i must have been a little girl
i must have had no thoughts
i don't feel beautiful anymore
i don't feel beautiful if you are dying
i look at my cat and don't feel beautiful
i hear music and don't feel beautiful
i read poetry and don't feel beautiful

* * *

i don't think i'll ever live by the ocean again
unless the ocean rises up in time
to meet me here
i think you would like it
in the place i grew up
people mainly want to drink there
you're always saying there's no time
like that episode of saved by the bell
where jessie takes caffeine pills

there are no good recipes
for cucumbers

* * *

i've been able to learn a few things:
politics are a lie
beauty is a lie
fame is a lie
my country is a lie
my father is a lie
i said eleven wrong things today
i stopped going to funerals
the pastor is a lie
the family is a lie
the corpse is a lie

* * *

some days i don't want to tell you
there are very dark ways to feel
i think i'll die
under a bridge
it's so easy to disappear
you just walk
until you can't see yourself

* * *

for my first eight years
i didn't know i was alive
then my grandma placed some butterflies in a jar
and their wings stopped
and we placed their bodies behind glass
sometimes when i'm alive now
i can't remember what i've said
but when i feel love
it feels like my heart could stop

SECTION II

ELIZABETH ACEVEDO

AN OPEN LETTER TO THE PROTESTERS OUTSIDE THE PLANNED PARENTHOOD NEAR MY JOB

who stuck a cross in my face and told me,
"abortions are the largest genocide of black people,
God won't forgive you for having one":

I'm not sure how I became the finger
to pull the trigger of your mouth.

That's a lie. I know exactly what turned
my lunch break into a firing range

and why this clay pigeon of a body
attracted your aim—
Tell me more, how you care about
"this largest genocide of black people"

when I've never seen you and your signs
at a Black Lives Matter protest.

Tell me, did you mourn Tamir & Aiyana & Jordan,
as hard as you celebrated the shooting of a clinic in Colorado?

Do you know how often I've walked by
your markers, megaphones, and mantras?

Your pickets signs and prayers that you cock like pistols
as I clench half a millennium of horror between my teeth?
You don't know my god.
You and mine   ain't on speaking terms.

My god understands the choices black women
have needed to make in the face of genocide.

My god understands how slave women plucked pearls
from between their legs rather than see them strung up by the neck.
My god doesn't condemn us who when faced with taking claim of our
bodies
do so with our chins unchained to the ground.

My god understands how for generations bodies like mine
were the choice for someone like you to make.
Do you know how many years, women like me
lived equally afraid of both hangings and hangers?
Yet we're still here, every day, carrying ourselves.

JOYCE PESEROFF

POEM BEGINNING WITH ITEMS FROM THE VIENNA MUSEUM OF CONTRACEPTION AND ABORTION

Rat poison.

A forty-pound rock.

Bundles of herbs.

A grapevine stalk.

Wire clothes hangers.

A scalding bath.

A tumble down stairs

or a granite cliff.

A forty-year sentence

in El Salvador.

Three felonies charged

by a Tennessee court.

She studied acting.

Almost failed trig.

Once hitched the moon

to the river's gig.

Go to another state.

Hope for another world

after they bounce you

from this one, girl.

SKIN II: FIREBIRD

A year after the last time he has come back
and I have left him, his markings on my body

deepened from darkened bruise to press
within nerve, tendon and bone

I meet a friend for dinner. Pulled
one by one from the oyster mouth

of her unclasped red handbag
she gives me lemons, yellow pearls raw
in the press of becoming

and I understand how the first creation
was not of water and newborn pink flesh

but out of ashed embers
ended, that single

red-risen flame.

RIB

between his stomach
and his heart

that place
taken from

other animals
and eaten

with barbecue
and applesauce

licked clean
and then thrown

to the dog

KWAME DAWES

BLACK FUNK

The rigid of my jaw bone
is power forged in the oven
of every blow I have felt.
My water walk is something like
compensation for a limp.
Don't begrudge me my sashay
walk, it's all I got sometimes.

'Cause I know the way you stare,
pale blue eyes like a machete edge
catching the colour of new sky,
the way you barely whisper
your orders, spit out the food,
complain about my shuffling gait,
snorting out my funky smell,
find fault in each task I do,
never right, never good enough,
curse my children like dogs,
cause I know you just hurting
drooling your bitterness
when my back is turned,

when the shape of my black ass
swings that way you hate,
sashaying through this room of daggers.

I know you're wondering what I've got
down there, in my belly, in my thighs,
make him leave your side,
crawl out of his pale sick skin
and howl like a beast at night,
whimper like a motherless babe
suckling on me, suckling on me

You can't hide the shame you feel
to know I sometimes turn him back.
I know you know it, from the way,
he comes on you hard and hurried,
searching for a hole to weep his soul in—
yes, I turn him back when I want,
and he still comes back for more.
I've got my pride sometimes.

I know the way you try to read me
try to be me, can't be me,
never be me, never feel the black
of me, never know the blues in me,
'cause you never want to see you
in me even though we bleed together,

finding each other's tidal rhythms
and bloat together like sisters,
hoarding the waters of the moon together

So I sashay through your life,
averting the blades with my leather skin.
I abuse you, and when he bawls,
that is my pride at work,
all I've got sometimes.
I'll cook your meals
until he keels over,
and you just have to take it
'cause I took it with no fuss
when he forced his nothing self on me,
while my babies sucked their thumbs
within the sound of my whimpering;
I paid baby;
I'm just reaping what y'all done sowed
Sometime I could sit down
and remember better
than I think I could remember—
from way back—better than I can do now.
I may say something today,
or see something today
or somebody may say something,
and it goes out.

GENDER

The first time I came
my heart faded quickly
and the plans of my father,
sensing the lifting of his load,
drifted away in a chill morning.
They planted my body,
my shriveled manhood,
curled like a worm.

When I came again,
castrated and thick-lashed,
my father counted his losses
and helped me grow the callous
of my hands, building
by his side the edifice
of our modest existence,
he did not see the coming
of my bleeding, man-child that I was.

But the boys could smell
the flaring of my womb,

could sniff their thirst-quencher
as I dragged the plough
through fallow ground. They would stare
at my cupped breasts as I ran,
leaping the low hedges of peanut bushes.
Their laughter, hands feeling at crotches,
tongues moistening the gleaming strands
of fledgling mustaches,
made me turn and run.

In the city, the wind played
whimsy with my bare thighs,
the soft fabric of my skin.
Here, the boys moved slower,
casual eyes recording me woman,
not taboo, homoerotic enigma,
simply woman walking the city streets
and my smile was big as light.

THE SECRET LIFE OF MARY CROW

Oh why the odor of decay sets the body/ trembling. We pretend we don't like/ sensitivity of the anus, smell of armpits./ After cooking, taking out the gar- bage—…Penis moving, among guts,/ membranes, juices. Gills of the vagina/ opening, closing.

—Mary Crow

I am happy to say my dreams of the ancient worlds have returned
When I went there with my cat mask on
Music for the sake of music
Snow that was not real
Water that is not
The bees
The secret life
And secret promises
We make to the dead
Before we move our way over
I moved the lantern, the desk
The freight train
Magic for the sake of it
I made the water black and gold

For you to swim in it, my love
But you were still a child
Not real
But released
Into another's arms
Almost for
An eternity
The secret life of Mary Crow
Is one where we are no longer us
But the beginning of things
Forever

*

I didn't go to the land of glittering lights
And cold mornings
To protect you
My baby Mary Crow
Who sits in my stomach
Fluttering its heartbeat
Like a wild boar
In the jungle of a bridge
The lights flashing
Before all the teenagers succumb to wounds
Inflicted by the family
Mary Crow, you've seen it all

And all the nostalgia of my youth
My life
Did not prepare me
For the next level over

*

The night came and went
Before I was supposed to go
We all have leaves
We are all under that milk sleep
At 6 o'clock in the morning
We all take a risk for love
Mary Crow, I'd never risk you
For the empty shtetl of my greatgrandmother
I'd never risk your heartbeat for the lonely flight of another halfway
    hello to everyone
I am looking for the real thing
Now I watch and watch under the red bridge
And I find the princess who was once you and isn't anymore
I understandably
Take my stead to the corner road
And knock upon the house of my bride
And say, Mary Crow
I am here
Won't you let me in

*

Maybe it's all fabricated
Maybe it's all a farce
The woman in the window is not Mary
We name her Susan or Syblance
We name her Anne
We got her a good stocking
Before we shoved the light out
I can't write anymore
I don't speak
The once twice beloved he writes me mantras to himself
But not full of blood
They are the flat sentences of his youth
They are the empty periods
That cut everything in two
They are everything I have always given up
To be another person
They are green daddy and rich mayabell
They are the poem after the person
I can still hear him reading in the dark
After they turned the lights out

*

When a person dies
They usually find the body on the floor

It's true
All things fall as low as they can go
I know I too have gone
Thud in the last bit
Not from carnal knowledge
But from my love of you
Which is vast and unknowing
Beyond book and crypt keeper
Which is beyond light
I know the striped clock
The ghost clowns keep before the dull chill
Right before they take your teeth out
And rock your corpse upside down
To see the teeth fall
I know the body is a corpse and text
But is also a possibility
I know all the things they said
I really listened, despite it all

*

In the early days my friend
Thinking of the embryo
Put a baby elephant in a sack
And sent a picture of it to me
The moon dream

Then a cheetah and a lion
He put a tiny baby in a balloon
I took my skin and packed it around me
And ate a tonic full of vegetables for health
To fill my veins with vitamins
You have to stay you say
And you stop up my blood with an unhealthy cork
And this you say, this is natural
Before you put to bed our dreams and hopes
And what they were for anyway

*

I know in that moment
When I reached the uneven hour
I thought of my own blood pulsing
And yours papery
Like a lance
Like something that doesn't go anywhere
Like my friend's big dick
Like the children's playing cards
I thought of tarot
Which is a kind of blood
And I don't have friends anymore
I just wait and watch
For the underscorer to make his match in the sun

The girls unapologetic for what they've become
My own sorry for not doing the job like I said I would
But what if I had known
The dreams that would befall
If I had only known
You Mary Crow
Would come into my life so suddenly
Oh Mary Crow
Mary Crow

*

In the uneven night
When I should have been on
The freight train, with my many colored packages
They said he got locked into stomach care
So I stayed in my empty room
I don't want to shit or dream
Til I have this thing inside of me
Which might be the woman
We all hold
Maybe I'll go
Maybe that's what's left of me
Maybe I will be quiet in the yellow
And no one will talk to me
Maybe I will finally go on a date

After all
With the wild German man
Who holds a golden cross
As a plan for all beginnings
Maybe there is not a beginning
Even I can hold

*

Music for the sake of music is what they say to you
When the cutting has begun
You are not you anymore
In this form
And if you made a baby that has transformed
From two things
You can make a thing that is many things at once
We struggle
To know this
It's just what is
Still such a loser you are
Still how the season has changed
And will never be again
And vulnerability is imminent
Like the stroke
Like when the brain blooms
Like when the sterile room

Like when they put the tulips in my room
I said, who are they from
And they were from myself in another life
So red and horrible
Against the white landscape
Of my sorrow

*

Mary Crow I told you I didn't want anything
But you came back instead
To make me a piece of you
Magic for the sake of magic
And the end
Which is slightly offputting
And the end which is like the night
But the dark and light is not the night
And the night which is not the end
And the beach in which we walked
So many lifetimes ago
I was another person
Actually
When I opened the door and said
This is new
And it was
And it's new
It's new again

THIS IS A SCREWDRIVER, SHE SAYS

pouring something called Smirnoff
into my Sunny-D and telling me
terrible things I can never unknow.
We get tired of Uno.
It's too hot, she says, and undresses,
room damp with the open-mouthed
memory of her ton of sleeping brothers—
a smell I can put my finger in:
sweet socks and peppered ham.
They share this mattress.
But they aren't home.
She stretches out in bluebell panties.
The window AC drips in my drink.
Thunder mutters in the distance.
She opens her legs. *You lost*, she says,
so this is your punishment.
Ew, I say, but I want to, and do.
Then it's time for her punishment.
Up above, the heavy cloud of her
teddy hammock threatens to burst.
We hear a door slam. We scuttle

to the closet. In the dark we're even
closer. My face in her crotch
and an old pair of Converse.
I don't think we can ever stop this.
But it's raining and her brothers
come back in from the court.
The closet opens and they catch us at it
like unearthed worms.
One of them throws a ball at us.
She curses at them in Spanish.
You raped our sister, says the tall one.
He looks like he believes it.
I try to find my shorts as they spit
and kick me. I'm so dizzy.
She was my friend. We were eleven.

CALIFORNIA KING

Behind closed doors, he bores me.
His frank, functional sensuality
lumbers across the too-big bed
like I am not Goldilocks, like I will
not leap up or eat up his lukewarm
porridge, not clutter up his cutlery.
Now knifing—   Now forking—
His utility ululates me, strains me
of stupid, so what do I care: mouth
full, brain blunted, body a wrung
knee-sock on the chair-back. *Wait.*
My whole world smells of marinara
& strife. See me spread butter.
See me spread eagle. See me keep
pleasing this rubber republican dick.
He talks dirty in fleece, but I bleat:
Have some almonds & cream sherry
O yes cream sherry! He shushes &
solves for X. Big teddy bear! Eyes like
flat buttons sewn-on & so what?

When I put my finger to his stitches,
he'll spill his Right Stuff on my runway,
touching secondary sex characteristics
like spots on some Twister mat:
right breast yellow, left testicle red,
another flick of the spinner? *O sure*.
In his Kingdom of Bore, how richly
he bores me, he bores me, he bores me!

KISS ME

Ruth Bader Ginsburg sits in the nineteenth row of my heart while onstage, a woman has been conscribed to the shape of a shrew. The actress has forty-carat eyes, an aquiline nose; her shoulders slight, her waist small enough. She is spanked over our hero's knee and I am laughing—everyone is laughing—except the conductor, who must steady his baton, and the house manager, who has seen it before, and the actors directed instead to be aghast, agape, gawking, agog, whatever Cole Porter rhymes with *dismayed*, and Ginsburg, who adjusts the pearl clipped to her ear. She curls the program in her lap. This is tiring, attending theaters of the heart. She doesn't relish it as Sandra Day O'Connor did, sipping champagne at the intermission of *Porgy & Bess*. The gangsters soft-shoe, reminding us to brush up on our Shakespeare. The actress sings "I am Ashamed That Women Are So Simple." Soon, Kate will be tamed. That's how we know the ending is happy.

DANIELLE CHAPMAN

LADIES WEEKEND IN BROOKLYN

Under a bright November sky a crowd of white
And Asian people flowed over the Bridge, so many
I had not known beards adorned so many
Of the young men, berets so many of the old
As they held up their selfie sticks and smiled
Against cables stripped as Scarsdale's hills
Of their last crackly red flare the color of my hair

While with my lady friends I strode, my hair
A Ukrainian prison shade of red (Ginger Mahogany
Kristina had said as distractedly I coveted her
eyebrow thread), helicopters whirring past the Statue—
Her—toward Battery Park's helipad, where the mad
Man's apricot chimp pelt lifted up, saluting
The city's glittery phalluses.

When from beneath the river's chalk-orange ferry,
The piers where new New Yorkers kicked penalties,
From the pale blue eyes of an Australian Terrier,
The boys' bodies curved into the OY, and theirs
Who poured over bridges with strollers

Just like ours, furze-green pashminas calyxing
The wisps fringing their crowns since pregnancy

A char ghosted up, through Pitt Street's megaliths,
Pinwheeled through sluices of real estate,
Living rooms keyholed in clocks of factories,
Mingled with actual mackerel packed in oil,
Pickles stilled in brine, and all the dim sum
Simmering among families picking foam buns
Truffled with burgundy pork the color of my hair dye:

It charred the clear Manhattan air, censored
By sanity and water taxis, Brooklyn's indoor carousel,
Grandiose in its transparency, the horses' painted faces,
Their rose-gardenia arses, fragrant and coarse
As adulteresses' to ISIS, or womanists to trolls
Even as I saw the pylons in a cove of café tables
Beheaded, at an angle, necks giving off an ordered zeal:

A fish-iron-and-fire smell of hatred for the chic
Rockabilly waitress, the stylist's hijab on the bias
Or any of us: one *blanc*, one *brun*, one far too red,
Hair flung out, faces slid into rictuses, hit, and hit again
By wind, here, there, everywhere, terrified, exultant, pure
With the endless, restless need of women to take pleasure
In womanhood even if it prophecies war forever.

SERVICE

Somewhere outside of Albuquerque, I was all

fed up with the stories about your ex-girlfriend's

Guess billboard in New York City, and to make

matters worse, I had to pee like a racehorse, or

like a girl who'd had way too much to drink

too far away from home. You stopped at a friend's

body shop to talk about a buddy who was stuck

some place in Mexico. You were talking, pulling

strings and taking pulls off a brown bottle, and no

one told me where the bathroom was, so I walked

back to where the hotrods were displayed like dogs

ready for a fight, baring their grills like teeth.

I was hungry, the air smelled like hot gasoline

and that sweet carnation smell of oil and coolant.

A girl pit bull came and circled me as I circled

the cars; she sniffed my ankles like I was her kin

or on some kind of rescue mission. You were still

talking, not a glance in the direction of me

and the bitch working our ways around

the souped-up Corvettes and power tools.

The pit was glossy, well cared for, a queen

of the car shop, and when she widened

her hind legs and squatted to pee all over

one of the car's dropped canvases, I took it

as a challenge. The strong yellow stream seemed

to be saying, *Girl, no one's going to tell me*

when to take a leak, when to bow down,

when not to bite. So, right then, in the dim lights

of the strange garage, I lifted my skirt and pissed

like the hard bitch I was.

DOWRY

i went home   i went missing
built a shrine to all my manmade hurts
my manmade limits my borders [i don't
like to be touched] i zip in & out of my
mottled body   smudged up in fingerprints
& in teeth   i reach for the saffron of
the light & paint myself   powder my
face with my homeland turned to dust
& all i've got in my hands are the infinite
variations of myself   a girl by another
name   looking down one day as my
grandmother did before me   to see my
hands wrinkling like rivers seen from above

SAFIA ELHILLO

ZIHOUR

bright scarves damp with the kitchen's heat   i measure myself against
the solid heft of bodies
tall & shaped in soft protrusions   forest of baobab
trees   i count gold bangles
from old dowries   submerged to the elbow in ground
meat   in young pink
waiting to be browned in fire   & always the thin gleam of
chatter rising above the hiss
of steam & searing fat   each mouth with the tincture of an
accent   its copper veins
filling the english used to address me   i am slim-hipped &
unmarried & sit childlike
shredding dill   & my arabic comes slowly & my hair is
unbrushed   but i work quietly
& pull the steam & smells in through my pores   & i am mothered
& grandmothered & held
close in the kitchen's breast

SAFIA ELHILLO

AFTER

after Danez Smith, with a line by Ol' Dirty Bastard

if you read this in red maybe i didn't
survive   every day i go missing   one
eyelash at a time   or sometimes   all
at once   & in the heaven for
blackgirls gone away   we walk in
& out of rivers & wear   our good silks
our good brown velvet bodies   dripping
with sunlight   we sprout leaves & no one
decides for us to cut or keep them   we
bear fruit & self-sustain   we tread water we
pluck the moon for our hair & another grows
in its place   we are sistered or unsistered
but never again to a dead thing   somewhere
a rope turns & turns & our feet never   touch
the ground   somewhere a song plays & plays
& names us with each touch of a needle to our
round black surfaces
i'm hanging out   */partying/with girls/that never die*

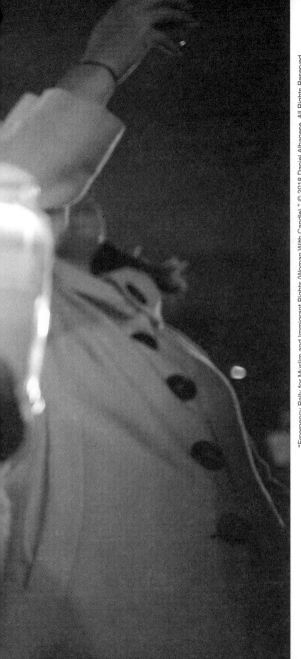

SECTION III

THE FOUR NIGHTS SHE'S GONE

I.

The news says two rapists
escaped from the state penitentiary.
Your friend's husband comes over
for dinner. He teaches your son to jump
the sprinkler in the yard. You drink gin
on the back steps, talk like two men do.

He eats spaghetti at your table,
the light settling behind the trees.
He stays when your son begs
for a movie, and the three of you
stretch out on the couch, the tv
fervent with little penguins.
Your son touches his beard;
you want him to spend the night
to stand watch at the door
in shifts with you, like soldiers.

You talk yourself down:

the rapists won't come here
you took thirteen years of martial arts
you know how to kill a man
they might not even be rapists

You do not ask him to stay.
You hear the helicopters overhead,
their lights scanning the neighborhood.
You scold yourself, as you put your son to bed.
What kind of man are you?
Maybe your son does need a father
if you are scared of a town jailbreak.

You sing to him,
the same song your mother sung to you.
You wonder what song
a real man would sing
or if the kind of man
who guards the door
would sing at all.

II.

You find out an alligator
has snatched a two-year-old boy

from a lagoon. They say
his father fought the alligator
for his boy; they say this time of year
is nesting season for the alligator,
guarding her young, protecting
the perimeter of her ninety eggs
which she listens to intently until
she hears a high-pitch of noise
coming from the eggs, which signals
she should uncover the nest.

You imagine yourself fighting
the alligator, your fists bloody
with the scrape of her claws
which, they say, are considered
lucky for gamblers. You imagine
you are able to kill the alligator,
That your rage is too great
even for a five hundred pound
reptile mother. You close your eyes.
You see yourself carrying your son
from the water, the alligator
floating at the edge, dead
instead of your son. Her young
left to be born lost. This
is what we do: imagine

our strength more holy,
our rage more pure,
our love some other-worldly force
impossible to contain, dangerous,
and beyond measure.

III.

The neighborhood
too quiet—its breath sucked
into summer heat.
Your son asleep too easily,
doesn't even call you back
doesn't plea for one more song
at the edge of his bed.

You sit still in a kitchen chair,
planted like a push pin,
staring into half-eaten dinner.

You don't clean the dishes.
You don't make his lunch.
You don't write anything down.
You sit perfectly still, like a child
who thinks *if I don't move*
then no one can see me.

IV.

You fall asleep on the couch
as you sometimes do when
she's out of town. 2 am,
the air conditioning quits on you,
the neighbor's dog barking
at its back gate. You wake up sweating.

You pull the steak knife from under the couch
(You've been carrying it from room to room).
You think to yourself: *a real man would have a gun.*

This night, in Orlando, there is a real man
with a real gun, who has just begun shooting
in a nightclub, on a dance floor, in a bathroom.
Presumably, protecting whatever it is
he sees fit to defend. But it turns out,
in the end, not everything broken
in him—in us—is worth saving.

EPITHALAMION

The wedding

is, as I have by now demonstrated, foretold.
It can't not happen. One is to one's shadow
as one's future is to one. And as attached.

Rituals

place one metaphorically among the women who came before us:
mermaid, princess, sheath, column, empire. The bouquet toss, in which
bride, now completed, predicts the next completion, eyes closed, back
turned. There is nothing old. I am not a virgin. Who will help me dress?
I have one mother and no father and one mother who was around once,
for a while, then left. I do not have the parts.

Ok: the night before, take all the food out of your refrigerator—lentils,
tomatoes, chocolate milk, chorizo, whatever—cook it and feast. Then,
instead of washing the pots and pans and hanging them back on the wall,
where they have always gone, take them out the front door and arrange
them by the curb. If they fill with rain, your marriage will be happy and
permanent.

Ceremony

If the wedding is foretold, it is therefore also only
a formality.

Like being announced as *for the first time.* Of course
this is not the first time.

Last summer my mother said *Weddings come and go.*
Like it's a rule—

Walking down the dark street beside you one night
my body blooms.

It opens. Just like that. Here's a rule: true union always
exists before it *occurs.*

More Vows

When I am with you I feel
I am not just myself, but rather
double myself, my consciousness
laid out one on top of itself like
a double-yolked egg, which is to say
auspiciously.
            I might therefore need
to vow myself to you. I love you
obsessively. I love you biologically.

I love you with sincere greed.
I am never doing this again.
Again, again.

Reception

Cover the walls with white sheets
and project Swedish pornography onto the ceiling.
As the night wears on, break potted plants open
and throw dirt everywhere, especially at your loved ones
—no. Rename everyone who walks through the door.
Their name is now George. Resurrect the great many misogynists
who bore that name. Invite only strangers. Serve only petit fours. No,
no: it is spring. Decorate with snow made of warm feathers,
order ice sculptures in the shapes of motorcycles
so the guests can ride, can feel the power
of a thousand pounds of frozen water
between their thighs! No! The theme
is Absolute Last Night On Earth.
At a party like that, you can't come back
once you leave. Everyone knows it's forever.
Which is the message you want to send. That's it.
That's the theme. Run with it! Run
with it. Cover the walls in butcher paper
and attach markers to the wall with festive ribbons

so your guests write their own epitaphs. This is the theme!
Bake it into a creatively-shaped cake and
smash it into your partner's face like,
here, eat it.

Recessional

And when we step off the porch, it is into
wet grass, the fireflies that never stop.

The columns of bodies holding sparklers.
Bodies which gave us life throwing rice.

The trail forward is laid out and well-marked,
even if it's not clear why. Even if, in the end,

the police come and find us, finally *see* us,
tell us we're illegal and take us in, violence,

the ground beneath our feet will swallow us.
The ground will swallow us tonight.

Night

Standing in the darkness
in the middle of the room
you say, *Well, can I take off my underwear?*

And though I'm not there to see it
happen, in the church down the street
the mouths at the height of the organ

begin to flap airlessly, to soundlessly
yawp, into the dark emptiness over
the bodiless pews—yes. Yes.

VORTEX TEMPORUM

We are not what we have loved.
We do not look like that thing we have loved.

And the unlearnable instrument is
the body attached to us. Though
I didn't know it until just now.

So I change my face. I make the room
dark, so that the person who positions themself between my legs
is also darkness. There is no pleasure.
"I" "want" "none."

With my eyes closed we could be holding hands
across the kitchen table in the night heat, our arms
sticking to its warped vinyl surface, while the bowl
with its six tomatoes sits between us, their enormous
redness pressed up against the glass as against

the open air. To live in a refrigerator saps tomatoes
of both taste and nutrients. Out in the air
I can almost smell them breathe.
And we listen. And the listening
seems to take no time at all.

WHAT SHE THINKS AS SHE WAITS BY THE DOOR

Alice Kramden of The Honeymooners

I was crafted, it would seem, to squeal demurely beneath
his shifting flab, to pucker my carnation lips on cue, to ladle
gobs of twice-boiled vegetables and stringy slabs of meat

into his grumbling yap. It would seem that way. After all,
the whole of my body is apron. I am always holding that
scorched pot, a bleached towel, a gray sopping sponge,

an iron, his huge hot folded trousers, a mop, a crusted dish,
a broom. I am always expertly positioned near the door
of this tenement hovel that's not much more than this single

room, my eyes wide and feigning joy, poised to drip sugar
around his blustering evening entrance. The air is decorated
with the words *control, control* while chunks of water grow

stale in the belly of the icebox. I am 1950s faultless, my pert
strawberry crown primly ponied. Never wore a dress that wasn't
a tribute to him. You don't believe I stood still and perfectly

upright for my wedding vows. Drowning in mama's wilting
taffeta, I was a bell: *I do, I do, I do.* And I did. With God and
a room of pouters as witness, I committed to a post-war, eerily

patient love. Beside me, splotched scarlet, he panted under
snug collar, a flowered tonic dripping from his curls. I could
have crashed his stunned smile with a finger. Someone said

God, then someone said *wife*, and I was so clarified I sparkled,
I was my own headspring of light, I arced toward the domestic
promise wiggling in flaccid fingers. I did not hear the word

fist. I was anxious to build romance, and I did. My lips found
the folds water couldn't reach. I gave him the name of a wall.
The first morning we rose from our separate untumbled beds,

our night skins pimpled and flushed with the prospect of touch,
was the first time he hefted his fist and threatened to send me,
Alice, to the moon, as if the moon was a definite, something

we could not only conjure, but find faith in. For years since
then, he has hefted that fist, it has brushed past my unblinking
eye, my chin, my clamped jaw, while the moon, uninterested,

is the same blaring yellow kink in our sleep. Screeching his
blind intent, *To the moon, Alice, to the moon!*, his eyes google
the lifted fist quivers, the spittle of his day needles my cheeks.

One of these days, Alice, one of these days! Bang! Zoom!
Without speaking, I show him who he truly is. I call stupid out
where stupid is. I'm mute while he spouts another craving wide
enough to fall through. Our tiled floor is littered with schemes,

his punctured zeal: *I'm gonna get a better job. Got a new idea,*
we'll be swimming in dough. Gonna take you out jitterbugging,
baby, buy you a dress, gonna turn our noses up to the hoi polloi.

I'm a champ at suffering his relentless inventions, concoctions
of spit and wood utterly guaranteed to drown us in new money.
What he can't say: *Baby, there's got to be something better*

than that bus, the smolder, the street disappearing beneath me.
I know he aches to give the slip to the same stream of the same
folded-face New Yorkers, all snarling and stank with factory,
nodding him their dead howdy-dos and clutching just enough
change to move themselves forward. *It's the cage of the ride,*
baby, every day like every week like every month like every year,

year like every and the wheels on the bus go round and round
and when he finally makes it home, to door, to this box, to *wife,*
he bursts in, sputtering some fresh grail, bound to clatter and rise,

and I am gingham and smelling of spray starch, my whole day
beneath my nails, I am twang and the wide-eye, *Really, Ralph?*
Really? I hold my breath, cramming his crave with stew meat

and ice water until it all comes exploding down, until he can't
turn his bulk in any direction without reaching a corner, until he
realizes, yet again, that his best friend stinks of sewage and, for

reasons we pretend to have forgotten, I am never ever naked.
And yes, I know what my practiced smirk practically begs him
to do—*Pow! Right in the kisser!* But that sweaty mitt, hovering

high with such sad engine behind it, will never fall. See, every
woman is damned with a man to raise, a swaggering snarl of belly
and bicep, and every ounce of the one I've been given cracks dulcet

beneath my held tongue and primp. I let the world burn brash
through him, because when he resurrects, when he yanks loose my
apron ties and mutters *Baby, you're the greatest*, it is still 1955, a time

of steam radiators and vows of stiff lyric, and he is everything a man
can be just then. I am *wife*. I am what the fist craves. And I am the fist.

THAT'S WHERE YOU DISAPPEAR

The kitchen towel absorbs the sweat
of steamed beans, splattered beet juice.

Into the gravy boat I pour *every man is a grave*.
For I have crammed all the names

of dirt into my mouth and dug my way
out with words as shovels.

Tonight I let fire grope the house.
Let the rats on the roof be

spelled backwards. Into the pan I burn
every man is a cloud-shaped bruise.

And yours, yours the contours of a country
no longer ours. I let the fire ruin

the curtains and rattle the windows.
The charred beans scatter across

the floor like roaches. On the chair
your coat with its puppet shoulders.

Your puppet show. Into the smoke I carve
every man is a smeared shadow of himself.

So tonight I let fire unbolt the doors,
and the trees on the block dance

like black-veined feathers. You're the void
between these lines. *Every man is a void*

between these lines. I lock your shadow
with its mothballs in the hallway closet

and let the fire suffocate what's left.
This house is no longer yours to shovel.

This house is no longer a grave.

AMANDA JOHNSTON

PHOTO: WHITE WOMAN SITTING ON BLACK WOMAN AS CHAIR ON MLK DAY

January 20, 2016

Once the image went viral in our minds, we were instructed
to find comfort in plush upholstered apologies neatly pressed and folded
like the woman, who was not a woman, *really*, a mannequin made to be
buckled
on her back, topless afro kink that didn't mean to offend, didn't mean
anything
because the artist had his reasons, *really*, because the woman sitting on
the lie
of a Black woman, her blonde hair neatly pulled back, starched white
shirt and pressed jeans were not a statement of superiority and context
matters here,
and power matters always, and I've never been to Russia so I wouldn't
know
this cover girl from a can of beans that costs less than what this magazine
wants

me to eat, but I know I'll pay for this in the end even though I'm not buying
the woman on the floor is a mannequin and not someone real struggling to find the exits, naked, in a room full of mirrors without reflection.

AMANDA JOHNSTON

WHEN MY DAUGHTER WASN'T ASSAULTED

She shook with fear, *or was it guilt*,
at the officer's unraised hand and smile.
How she leaned away, slowly, when he called
a tow truck instead of backup.
How her tears fled when he showed mercy
over rage for the couple on the side of the highway,
flat tire wasted against asphalt. She couldn't help
but look at her white boyfriend pacing
along this strip of road and wonder, what if
this was a different part of Texas?
What if this hero was a different shade of power?
Would she be so lucky, *or was it luck*,
if the absence of a known pain
is just a heavy hand in repose?

IT WAS THERE! NOW IT'S GONE. NO, WAIT THERE IT IS

your orbit reaching down down down
supernova revolting & you never even
wanted to be a star. shine. glow. spin.
all your roots up up & away. we go. on
like nothing is quaking as if the ground
is steady as she goes & om but you know
the trembling is happening si(lent)ly you
know the magnitude is not worth trying
to let me tell you let me tell you let me tell
you. wash your di(she)s differently now like
babies like ducks like if you break a dish
this will not mean good luck like if you
crack a mirror you can't have the maybe
of 7 years eating away at your nipples.
baby. you wish you could hold yourself
& knit yourself a blanky. nuzzle yourself in
the idea of mama won't let a thing hurt
you. your orbit reaching down down down

supernova revolting & you never even
wanted to be a star. shine. glow. spin.
all your roots up up & away. we go.

ELEGY WITH A WHITE SHIRT

The way we waited for the year to end

made me think of walking backward under a mandrake
sky, cloth rough and hot with my own breath on my cheeks

as the hill began to resemble an eyelid,
the line of men in black, shields pressed side by side like a howl

spelled out, its lashes.

In the solid lake, one of the shadows had started a fire; heavy things
spilled across the asphalt. I remember thinking

I knew what violence was: verdicts left under stones

in my body and how recondite
the shapes I could fold into at the imagined end of an arrow which
    appears

as a train writing the red of gone

on glassy spines; how
electrifying, those veins appearing in the window, the city's false
sleep, lashes separating as they swept down

toward the dark mass in which I was
one strand of smoke.

••

That was years ago, in another country,
where as a rule, people carried rain inside

them like small hammers.

In Orozco's *Combat* a blade is thrust through the suggestion of a body

inside a white shirt. I see a fist pushing
the blade in, and the blade coming clean through

the bracket where the ribs should be. There is no blood.
The shirt is holding

a line with other shirts like a wave
cresting backward against its own dark sea
pounding from the opposite shore,
suggesting an endlessness to struggle and within, fire's

vanity. From behind, I see what the white shirts cannot: faces

afloat in the umbrage of raised blades, trying to make
their way here. Maybe I am trying

to make my way there. It is not always clear

these days whether between here and there, I am supposed to break or
hold the line.

• •

In my homeland, the people wear white to signify readiness to die.

My homeland lives like a witch in my house, turning the rice
yellow and filling my mouth with marbles

when my mother calls. She puts up strange lights
in the air of my mind; sometimes they bark like dogs and when

the mask of gasoline sticks too zealously, I pause my breath to lick it.

Under the white shirt, the wound is longer
than any blood. Under the parade of the pure, the wind-defying

veils of redemption, my bones suggest spill.

                    I dig around them
day and night for the poem as irrigation; myself

as probable. Which is to say here, not there, a fleck of bloodless
on the bomb-encrusted *we*

        some call necromancy and others,

America.
I've never seen the witch in my house in a white shirt.

I've never seen her write. But her verdict I feel
behind every line, burning

• •

or not. For instance, mingling ashes with snow, wondering
where "my" portion of pavement begins and if today

the kids at Berks Family Detention Center are wrapping bandages

around their own snow-people.
Kids whose cards to Santa have found *The Guardian*
instead, questing that old burglar—pinnacle of red in whom grows fat

our love for the obsolete like wet
                              fruit in jaws of snow—*para*

la libertad. The iron-clad
irony sticks in an old hole in my ribs. On white paper, neon-
colored squiggles, erratic lines suggest

stars,
flowers,
small
hands of endless sea.

FRANCINE J. HARRIS

ANISE SWALLOWTAIL, MOULTING

He says *papillon* and you want to take
his word for it. The thorax is missing its yellow wing.

What do you say when that happens. *Muer.* he says. He says you thought
    it meant
woman. But no, he says, and his chin. The slender proboscis drinks
    nectar.

Like a straw, you say. Yes, he says. Has one ever fallen on your sweat in
    summer.
won't always get enough salt, from flower. The ocean, you think. Alive,
    he says

they are hidden in tree limbs, mimic the bark. You think: yeah, but the
    trees here
are rotten and burned. and it looks like a moth, torn. Others, he says,
    sniff the air for stem.

You want to ask: how many fingers to tear up the butterfly. But you know
    he'll say
if they are only children, it does not count. You would smoke from the
    wingtip

and flame the wing. You say the sun is shot here. Everyone's on edge. He says

any excuse, you'd trap butterflies in tupperware and ask strangers dumb questions like:

What do you call it when a dead thing's wing comes off? You say you'd tell someone anyway.

You say you'd get the crying over with. If it was a little girl in dirt, touch her sun-edged hair.

Tender he says, what doesn't know how to treat limb's fruit. The same to you. You want the one

in the bowl who has lost her articulated flutter. To stand up to the claws. To fight back. He says,

you'd still snuff it out. Ask any one. You say: your french words make me feel bad. You should

ask if he means it. If he means *papillon* you. Is he thinking of a dead one. one

that smells of fennel. What would he have called it when he was a boy

in the dirt. tearing wings in the dirt. He says, well then. then, who do we blame.

ROSEBUD BEN-ONI

AM HA'ARETZ

In the gardens of givat ram
We never saw
Solomon's turtledoves
For seven years the winter
And the rain   she and I
Strangers in the midrahov   she and I
Cracked cobblestone
Once a market road
Deserted on a sabbath evening
All the jackals are gone
And every day in july
Tempting that last stretch of sky   she and I
The end so close   we lied
Beyond reach   somewhere the mountains in the
          mountains
Among lotus shrubs   she and I never saw
Wild goats rising up
Or grackles
Picking off the parasites   and what of those nights
In the snow in the snow

Sweeping the midrahov
Those nights when I was repossessed
By am ha'aretz
After I lost her
In ammei ha'aretz
    These roads I do not know I do not know
                          her arms anymore her arms
                              all the children's songs
                    sowing
          her tongue   she and I
              those lost gardens of the desert
                  that die each night
in ammei ha'aretz

Author's Note: In the Hebrew canon, "the people of the land" (the singular *am ha'aretz*) refers to the Jews. The plural *ammei ha'aretz* refers to foreigners, or non-Jews living within Eretz Yisrael.

ELIZABETH CLARK WESSEL

1991

Do you remember the Gulf War?
Do you remember what it looked like on TV?
Flashes of bright green across a dull green background.
Scud. Rockets.
More abstract than Super Mario Brothers.
A classmate's brother wrote home,
we're living in a palace these days, sleeping on marble floors.
I imagined a floor made of thousands of marbles,
thought how uncomfortable that would be.
The whims of kings are inscrutable, I guess.
That was the year I watched Ken Burns' *Civil War* on a loop.
I loved the pictures of battlefields before and after,
peaceful then pockmarked and perfectly decrepit.
I loved how Gettysburg was saved by a textbook every time.
That was also the year someone cooked meat in strychnine
and threw it to dogs all over town.
First they'd foam at the mouth,
then shudder, then die.
It happened to my dog.
I saw it.

She was a birthday present, and I used to wake up early
to feed her puppy chow softened in hot milk.
I warmed it up in the microwave
and went out to the little garden shed where she slept.
This is the order of things.
First one thing, and then the other.
It's taken me a long time to understand this.

ELIZABETH CLARK WESSEL

A WOMAN AND HER JOB

A woman takes a subway to its last stop, then a bus to its last stop. She walks four blocks to her job, teaching English at a preschool for the children of diplomats from China, Belgium, Korea, Finland. The woman is almost a child herself. At lunchtime she cooks macaroni for them. Cuts up cucumbers. Afterwards they all walk down to the water to see the geese, because they love to see the geese. They point and call the geese by the names they know for them, and the woman says geese, goose, gander, egg, water, geese, geese. Some of the children pick up one of these words and throw it at the lake like a stone. Later, on the lawn in front of the school, she teaches them ring around the rosy. They all love spinning in a circle as fast as they can. They all love they all fall down. Now the children start to say the words along with her, not knowing what they mean. Pocket full of posy. Ring around the rosy. The woman thinks, after today they will always know this song, but they won't know why, won't know it's because of me. Just like she's forgotten why or who. The littlest one, the one who knows the least, loves falling the most. Springtime is here now in the far north. Green green grass. The woman will know these children a few weeks more, and then she'll find another job. These children will live in this country a year or two more, and then they'll move somewhere else. This is what it is to live a modern life, thinks the woman, who is barely a woman, carrying things around everywhere and not knowing why or where they came from. The sun shines. Springtime has come now in the far north. The woman can't seem to find the connections between anything. The parents start to come and pick up their children one by one. Little backpacks are put on little backs. A brief word or two is exchanged in the perfect English of the parents and in her Midwestern English. The children chatter, so relieved to be understood. After the last child goes home, she walks to the bus. Only immigrants ride the bus in this expensive suburb, she thinks, looking around at the other immigrants on the bus. She rides to the subway. She rides the subway to her stop. She walks three blocks to her apartment. She unlocks the door and goes inside and opens all the windows. Springtime has come to the far north. When will the man she loves come home from the office? She climbs out the window into a garden. Her cat runs back and forth in ecstasy, chasing something she can't see. She reads a fat book by a Russian, while drinking something sweet. She keeps rereading the same sentence over and over again. At some point soon, the woman will finish reading this book, and she'll think about it all summer, talk about it all summer, even to people who aren't interested at all. At a party, just before she gets too drunk, she'll finally understand something profound about it and tell it to the woman sitting next to her. But all she'll remember later is that that woman didn't consider herself a feminist. She will feel the borders of herself constricting. Not today. Springtime has come to the far north. Bloom and bloom and bloom.

NATURALIZATION STUDY

You have not had any thoughts regarding art for approaching three
    months
This is perhaps a consequence of the law
This is perhaps a consequence of the unknowable quality of the genesis
    of the law
You feel displaced and your displacement relates inextricably to the
    displacement of others
I desire a handful of order, asking if you see me with any real affection
The most combative of us have perhaps been spit on the most
To be honest: this is a difficult way to begin
Punishment has departed the body and comes looking for the spirit
I shore up my psychic spaces
Around me I feel there is an unambitious orbit of facts
When I accept them they are totalizing
Who is for what in a closed egalitarian loop?
My mom places her hand on the white hot book
My mom presses her color into the declarative sentence ("the big cat is
brown") to show you what
you want to know
Life, my friends, is a salt lick you tongue repeatedly

The sanctity of being principled and every few years aggressively
    trimmed back
They put you on a list and said that your collection was an honor
They named you after a lily white flower
It was like a dream of spiritual refurbishment, delicately, strangely

RUTH IRUPÉ SANABRIA

ON *MATE* & THE WORK

If you are true,
knife the phallic gourd.
Gut it & cure it.
Prepare it for drink.

If you are true,
allow me to choose
the yellow silicone
over the wild & humid *porongo*.
Allow me to drink from it.

Refugee exile
immigrant witch
estupida pendeja
puta bitch
dyke cunt
mala
madre, madre
mala
& with each hunt,

injured
even if
not caught.

How are you?

This *mate*, it's dish washable.
Bought it on Amazon.

This little grandmother
was ordered to pull down her paintings
because the Rabbi was offended
by her version of Eve: 9 months pregnant,
unbroken & reaching for another apple.

This little grandmother,
with the word *¡escuchá!*,
from prison, smuggles a poem to her daughter:
as is a seed,
as is a drop of water
we are bound
to a triumphant bloom,
& my joy is entangled
with that of my brothers & sisters;
& I couldn't abandon this love.

How to fill the cellular hunger for one's mother, if one's mother is
    running?

What if one's mother is detained?
What if she is never the same, but one's hunger hasn't changed?

This little grandmother
sent her daughter to Juarez with money
to be given specifically to a mother searching
for her daughter who had been kidnapped & murdered in Juarez,
& specifically for the testimony she was giving
about her daughter kidnapped & murdered in Juarez
this mother was marked for death,
but she became 1000 mothers more.

Mates made of gourds steady palms.
Mates made of gourds remain composed.
Mates made of gourds hold the memory of touch.

This little grandmother
said the words plainly:
La triple jornada,
the triple shift:
at dawn the fork,
then the long obedience of the dollar
& after it is done,
and after dinner is done,
& the lover is loved, the dogs fed, &
as the children sleep
the work of justice and art begins

& her daughters understood.

Honey, syrup, or plain?
Boiled eggs or fried?
Two ponytails or one?
Breath, teeth, ears: check, check, check.
Lunch box, homework, sign & return,
dishwasher, laptop, phone,
car keys, house keys, chargers,
apples, waters, & I.D.s,
love you, love you, love you, listen
to your teachers, be kind, & remember,
listen isn't always the same as *shut up,* & remember
that the eye of the witness disarms the devil.

You can find this work, right here,
in the neighborhoods of your conscience.

Where can I find my eyes?

Silicone *mates* fall
& return upright & whole;
the fissure, a sorrow belonging
to the skull and its brain,
to the earth, her shells and her gourds.
Silicone *mates* travel unnoticed,
bent into themselves in the oppressive bulk

of crowded backpacks and hurried suitcases,
reshaping themselves like nothing.

What knot do you use to not fly away?
What is your mantra to keep your feet in line?
What is your anchor?

Never allow the water to boil.
Shake the *yerba* of its dust before pouring the first round.
Spit out your first sip.

Inspiration never comes over for *mate*.
Inspiration takes hours to get anything done.
Mostly, inspiration prefers to stay away
until you're almost done with what it is you called her for.

This little grandmother serves her husband *mate*:
Three sips at 4 o'clock every single day.
This little grandmother takes her *mate* alone,
after her husband has gone.
This little grandmother serves her husband *mate* in bed
before leaving to work.
This little grandmother is not bothered by you, little boy. You are fully
integrated into her skin, her book, her breath, & she drinks maté in a
sloppy American way: forgetting to shake the herb of its dust, forgetting

to spit out her first sip, giving you a sip of it while it is still strong,
throwing the silicone gourd in the dishwasher.

Not my daughter. What other offering, sky? Not my daughter.

Mind the kettle. Share the straw without fear.
If there is a sore on the lip or a cold in the lungs,
wipe the straw with a cloth & continue to share.

What are hands for? What are feet for? Heart? Voice?
We ask again & again.

Woke, mouth closed howling, industrious & on task.
To-do list scrolling down my back.

Thursday morning mother emptiness wakes me with a start, & drills
itself into my left hip. My floors are gross, the wastebasket is growing a
pool of blue mint, & I know you have some heart-balm. Friday night I'm
pushing the cart through Shoprite; days show up & I'm unprepared, the
walls are unfinished, there are nails sticking out, my roots are visible, my
fingers are raw. It is Monday & the toilet is disgusting. It is Tuesday &
I promise to pay when I am paid. Then, it is Wednesday, oils & bubbles
in the water for the children, coconut for their hair. Thursday, I do not
want to teach another unit on genocide. I am teaching another unit on
genocide. Friday. Mother. But you are a bonfire, & when low, flame.

30 years ago: you sit at your handmade desk, working
but available to me for talk about some aspect of your life & some aspect
    of mine.
Now, I sit in the car & I scroll to find your name.
But I swallow the ocean back. I am tidying up.

In this dream, I attend a conference of writers and professors.
You are dead. A woman reads from you.
She says you said that I said,
"use a word to use a word"
& this is how
by not abandoning this work, we don't abandon each other.

Once upon a time, a turtle took several decades to cross the street,
to get itself up the side of the house,
through the back door, into the living room,
to stare at you and you were mortified.
How the fuck did this monstrosity of determination
make it in without me noticing?

RACHEL ZUCKER

HOURS DAYS YEARS UNMOOR THEIR ORBITS

for my son

tonight I'm cleaning baby portobellos
for you, my young activist

wiping the dirty tops with a damp cloth
as carefully as I used to rinse raspberries

for you to adorn your fingertips
before eating each blood-red prize

these days you rarely look me in the eye
& your long shagged hair hides your smile

I don't expect you to remember or
understand the many ways I've kept you

alive or the life my love for you
has made me live

RACHEL ZUCKER

AND STILL I SPEAK OF IT

I did not see the sky today
it does or does not matter why

I sat inside & looked away
into the North-facing light of
what I can't won't shouldn't say

a girl I know of wants to die
I called the school I called her home

her father thanked me & hung up
the schoolman said *The world is hard*
harder for girls than it ever was

What a beautiful day Dan texts
I know nothing about it I respond

coming up next: The World
        but first: The Takeaway

the radio in my kitchen keeps itself company
muted drilling outside the window

a girl jumped from her grandmother's roof
one block from here & the doorman found her

her parents papered the building with letters
asking no one to speak of it

the United States cares about mankind
says the Brigadier General in my kitchen
it would have to include hostage negotiation
says a voice in my kitchen

says   *those taking part in the rebellion*
                           are called belligerents

says   *God instructed the man to sell the girls*

says   *get the girls back just get them back*
                       just get them back get them back

I sit very still & do nothing say nothing
am nothing & it is still too late

JANUARY, AFTER EL NIÑO

Dear child, as I write this, it is raining
in a city where it never rains.
People drive quickly, sloppily, angrily.
Surging around corners,
where people leave the Metro bus.
Where someone pushes a shopping cart,
then yanks it back before a pickup rushes by.

In this rain, I wish
that you should never want to go outside.
That I could read you stories, make you soup.
I wish you would never outgrow this room,
forever watch Thomas the Train,
Spill your Rice Krispies, toss Fisher-Price blocks.

I hear another car door slam, another horn blare.
Someone yells faggot,
and I wish you would remain an infant,
tiny feet in drawstring booties, that I
could shield with arms and back from the storm
and whatever ill it brings. To this world,

in which I wish you might never be born,
not now, when water fills like hatred
in the cracks and potholes of the roads,
inciting the voices, the wheels,
the engines that assault them every day. I wish,
this body had never opened,

that this heart had never known love,
that instead of you, what falls from above
would find no one to endanger, no one to hunger,
no one to harm.

SECTION IV

MARY RUEFLE

WOODTANGLE

I remember the king passed massive amounts
of inarticulate feeling into law.
I envied all the beautiful things.
Sometimes I called my own name.
I cursed myself why do I have so many
strange questions. I tried to cram myself
with gentler things so as to release
some suppressed inclination. My name is
Woodtangle. I remember my mother
when she wore yellow was beautiful
like a fish and then she died. I remember
thinking my father was mean but knowing he
was kind. I remember thinking my father was
kind but knowing he was mean. I remember thinking
all things made of themselves examples of the
same thing. And Everyman the next day would follow.
I remember thinking the world ended a long time ago
but no one noticed. I remember every dinner
at Vespaio with Tomaz and the Saturday night
the antique cars paraded by for any hour

And I couldn't breathe for the fumes and I was happy.
I remember thinking the sexual significance of
everything seemed absurd because we are made of
time and air (who cares) and then I remembered
the day the king passed massive amounts of inarticulate
feeling into law he threw a cherry bomb into the crowd
and I thought it was fruit and ate it.

RACHEL MCKIBBENS

SHIV

///

November 14th.
In the coffee shop,
the man in the
Make America Great Again hat
smiles at me, so I take this
as an invitation.

"Pardon me, but I have to ask—
do you think Trump's
ideologies keep every person
in this country safe?"

He doesn't hesitate.

"Ma'am, I can't get wrapped up
in identity politics, all I can
worry about is how
I'm going to feed my girls."

///

At my 40th birthday party,
an acquaintance asks
why we have "so much
Mexican art in the house."
"It might be because I'm Mexican," I say.
"No," he laughs, "you're not Mexican."
"Yes. I am."
"No," he continues, reassuringly,
"and if you are, you're only, maybe, 17%."
The winter air stiffens between us.
An old, familiar pain.

///

There was a time when I
would have thanked him.
The early years,
when I wanted only to pass,
to rid myself of my last name—
the dead giveaway,
its muddy lineage
crawl out from the burying shame
that held me down every time
my father picked me up
from school in our shitty car,
his bushy mustache

& brown face
magnified by the sun.

///

A local white woman
posts a photo of her new tattoo:
a Mayan god etched eternal
on her flesh. When I point out
the disrespect, she assures me
she speaks Spanish fluently,
spent three years
in South America.

For the next six hours,
I argue with her friends.
They demand I quit being so
divisive. Judgmental. Close-minded.

"We have a racist running for President,
and you're complaining about a tattoo?"
asks the white boy, who spray paints
murals all over this city
with impunity.

O, to be permitted the luxury
of only worrying about one thing at a time.

O, to be white in America,
to wake up knowing every god is your god.

///

When you never see yourself,
you search for yourself all the time.

You know the white girl
in the sombrero isn't you.
The bro dude in Calavera makeup
isn't either, not the ponchos
and glued on mustaches,
not the lowrider Chevy
in the Disney movie
or the hoochie-coochie
sex pot on the Emmy
award-winning television show.

Maybe you are only this:

the scorched bird pulled
from the chimney,
covered in soot.
Not the actual bird,
its velvet sack
of jigsaw'd bones,

but the feeling
of recognition.

The ash of knowing.

///

A white comedian tells this joke:
"I used to date Hispanics,
but now I prefer consensual."

The audience laughs.
And you do, too.
Until the punchline hardens,
translates into a stone
in your throat.

You swallow it, like you always do.

You don't change the channel,
but you also can't remember
a single joke she tells after that.

A few months later, the comedian's career
blows up. She's so real. So edgy.
Such a hardcore feminist.

When someone writes an essay on

her old stand-up routines—
noting her blindspot when it comes to race,

her response is:

"It is a joke and it is funny.
I know that because people laugh at it."

///

If two Mexicans are in a car, who is driving?
A police officer.

How do you starve a Mexican?
Put their food stamps in their work boots.

What's the difference between a Mexican and an elevator?
One can raise a child.

What do you call a Mexican baptism?
Bean dip

How do you stop a Mexican from robbing your house?
Put a help wanted sign in the window.

What do you call a Mexican driving a BMW?
Grand theft auto

What do you call a Mexican without a lawnmower?
Unemployed

What do you call a building full of Mexicans?
Jail

How do you keep Mexicans from stealing?
Put everything of value on the top shelf.

What do you call a bunch of Mexicans running downhill?
A mudslide.

Why don't Mexicans play Hide 'n Seek?
No one will look for them.

What does a Mexican get for Christmas?
Your TV.

What do you call the Arizona man shot to death
by his white neighbor, screaming, "Go back to Mexico!"
Juan Varela

///

November 29th.
For weeks, I've avoided
eye contact with strangers.
My face is a closed curtain.
My mouth, the most
decorated knife.
I pay for groceries,

grab the receipt &
let my half-hearted
thank yous trail like smoke.
I no longer want to see
who refuses to see me.

Anyone is everyone.

///

December 1st.
I keep waking up.
There isn't anyone
white enough to stop me.

Pantomime the living until
the body remembers:
wicked bitch. Bloodwhirl.
Patron Saint of the Grab Back.

Still. Still. Still. Still. Still. Still here.

///

I etch my own face upon my wicked flesh.
I am my own devastating god.

HAGAR IN THE WILDERNESS

Carved Marble. Edmonia Lewis, 1875

My God is the living God,
God of the impertinent exile.
An outcast who carved me
into an outcast carved
by sheer and stony will
to wander the desert
in search of deliverance
the way a mother hunts
for her wayward child.
God of each eye fixed to heaven,
God of the fallen water jug,
of all the hope a vessel holds
before spilling to barren sand.
God of flesh hewn from earth
and hammered beneath a will
immaculate with the power
to bear life from the lifeless
like a well in a wasteland.
I'm made in the image of a God

that knows flight but stays me
rock still to tell a story ancient
as slavery, old as the first time
hands clasped together for mercy
and parted to find only their own
salty blessing of sweat.
I have been touched by my God
in my creation, I've known her caress
of anointing callus across my face.
I know the lyric of her pulse
across these lips... and yes,
I've kissed the fingertips
of my dark and mortal God.
She has shown me the truth
behind each chiseled blow
that's carved me into this life,
the weight any woman might bear
to stretch her mouth toward her
one true God, her own
beaten, marble song.

IF 2017 WAS A POEM TITLE:

1.

When they turn bodegas into boutique grocery stores
When they bounce cops up the block
Like this hipster protection program won't turn back
Lefrak into Harlem turn back Harlem into Chirac
turn back BedStuy into Brownsville turn Brownsville back
Into the Bronx back into Gaza back...

You will taste this strange and bitter American history

Where the Mom and Pop work more hours than the Governor
Where the pesticides overflow our sewer systems
Float our food deserts into neighborhoods
One way in
One way out
Tell me this gentrification be for my own good
Tell me this housing project keep us warfare ready
Tell me Biggie died for our sins
& I'll show you a Brooklyn stoop with a babies' name etched in chalk
A hashtag ghost gone already

A price tag on his sisters face
She's been missing since Sunday
Where choppa lights paint concrete a trail of breadcrumbs
A haunting finding its way back to our homes

1.

> The Electoral College is
> a lullaby designed to put us
> back to sleep.

1.

The ocean is weeping a righteous rage, she got questions for the living:
& what about the sweetheart who would grow to love Tamir Rice?
Mike Brown? Korryn Gaines? Akia Gurley?
What about they mamas singing their name before each breakfast?
Or the church praying for their redemption—bibles raised in the air?
What about their (almost) children? How about they Daddy's smile?
What about they name make them so easy to turn to ash?
How we ghosting black boys for the toys we gift them?

1.

On a Monday
A white body told my black body

It ain't earned no apology for the bloodshed
For the nights when my skin grow so cold
I know I must be inches from death
For each death hand delivered to me,
    this: silence   this: certain dismissal   this: post racial reality show
    this: confederate hug
& don't it bloom like a mushroom sky?
What about the blues? Why it cry like hail?
Why it hell like America so so long

1.

Yo: America

Whatchu know about noose ready
Whatchu know about chalk lines & double barrels
Whatchu know about a murder weapon
Or a loose cigarette
Or a baby sleeping on a couch

Whatchu you know about the flag
The truck that followed me down a lonely road in Georgia
The names that I rolled off my tongue in prayer?

Saint Sojourner
Saint Harriet
Saint Rekia
Saint Sandra

Bring me home

Or leave me steady
Gun aimed and cocked ready

Con artists turned 45th resident of the White House
While the 44th President is lifted off the grounds
          by his shadow & his Black wife
She truth slayer all day
She cheekbone slay

Still the media aim and shot at presidential legacy
Until weed smoke & a concert make us remember
BLK people ain't never been human here

Ain't we beautiful?
Those that survived the purging ?
Those that spill, body splay beautiful from a hateful song?
This swing sweet sweet low spiritual ain't neva been inclusive

Whatchu know about larynx & baton
How you sing him crow in the key of Emmett Till
What fever fuss you awake?
Who else got cop'd anxiety?
Call it what it is: post traumatic slave syndrome
Call it land tax until homeless
Call it abortion turned sterilization
Ain't no lie like the one against our stillborn children

Ain't no lie like the many that shaped our babies into mute cattle
Prison industrial complex
reverberates in the tune of elementary
      4th graders are the easiest targets

1.

A Math Problem:
If 1 woman got 7 Mac 11's
& 2 heaters for the beemer
How many Congress seats will NRA lose?
How many votes will it take for a sexual predator
        to lift the White House off her feet?

1.

I am practicing this aim
This tongue a shoestring strafe

    Melt the wires of Guantanamo
    Yasiin Bey coming home ain't what we thought it would be
    Ain't no solace in Mecca
    Even Spike Lee left Brooklyn
    Here, a slumlord will leave my front steps
    Full of rat piss & AirBnB my neighbors' apartment
        for half my take home pay

Unhinge the city of Rikers
Bring back the reapers
Give them the loot & the stoop

Yea, they good at killin' but so was Jefferson.
I mean Washington. I mean CIA. I mean Cointelpro.
I mean they mimic your Grace. I mean it's 2017, America.
A new *new* year & your face lift be botched.

HERITAGE

Reyhaneh Jabbari, a 26-year-old Iranian woman, was hanged on October 25th, 2014, for killing a man who was attempting to rape her.

the body is a mosque borrowed from Heaven   centuries of time
stain the glazed brick   our skin rubs away like a chip
in the middle of an hourglass   sometimes I am so ashamed

of my sentience how little it matters   angels don't care about humility
you shaved your head   spent eleven days half-starved in solitary
and not a single divine trumpet wept into song   now it's lonely all over

I'm becoming more a vessel of memories than a person   it's a myth
that love lives in the heart   it lives in the throat we push it out
when we speak   when we gasp we take a little for ourselves

in books love can be war-ending   a soldier drops his sword
to lie forking oysters into his enemy's mouth   in life we hold love up
    to the light
to marvel at its impotence   you said in a letter to Sholeh

you weren't even killing the roaches in your cell   that you would take
    them up

by their antennae and flick them through the bars into a courtyard
where you could see men hammering long planks of cypress into gallows

the same men who years before threw their rings in the mud   who
    watered them
five times daily   who shot blackbirds off almond branches
and kissed the soil at the sight of sprouts   then cursed each other
    when the stalks

which should have licked their lips withered dryly at their knees   may
    God beat
us awake   scourge our brains to life   may we measure every victory
by the momentary absence of pain   there is no solace in
    history   this is a gift

we are given at birth   a pocket we fold into at death   goodbye now
    you mountain
you armada of flowers   you entire miserable decade in a lump in my
    throat
despite all our endlessly rehearsed rituals of mercy   it was you we sent
    on

POEM FOR SUHEIR HAMMAD

"I am a tunnel," she said,
        Meaning, not the route to her beloved Brooklyn,
                Home a way from
        Meaning, a thing you bomb, some
                    thing exploded.

Reuters runs photos,
        Of the aftermath
      (what is after math… when some thing
        Has happened… many things happened, but
    …there is no end in sight.
        What is the math of after, its calculus?)

Reuters runs photos
    Here are two women, sitting on the rubble
        (what is rubble?
            These were homes)

Sitting in the Rubble, what were homes in Rafaah
    Homes near tunnels
        Two women lived, near
                tunnels, meaning

A lifeline of food and medicine,
Or   something you bomb,
                        a thing exploded.

I am, she said,
    though borne into demolition

LAUREN K. ALLEYNE

ODE TO THE PANTSUIT

You thought yourself retired, lounging

unused in the back of 70s feminist closets

or retro thrift shop racks in all your iterations—

jackets, shoulder-padded, double-breasted, collars

sculpted into every shape of wing, embracing

your namesake boxy or slim-legged bottoms;

pantsuit, you thought your work was done.

You thought to retire, having served us well,

we women who donned you like armor

and strode proudly into spaces too spiked

for dresses, too fragile for the curve of leg

you held with such ease. You cloaked us

with confidence, the cape to every superheroine

wanting to kick in a glass ceiling. You

were the anti-cute, 'unflattering', a revolution

with functional pockets. Draped in you,

unladylike one, we slipped minds first

into a world that believed us hollow.

How you held our softness secret,

shielded our vulnerable with your badass.

Grab deflector. Pussy protector. Pantsuit,

you stayed with us, evolving as we did

into weaponized powersuited style,

blossoming into separates, daring silk

camisoles, frilled blouses, before long,

skirts. That must have been a blow,

but O pantsuit, you understood. Perhaps,

like so many of us you thought the battle over,

victory, if not immediate, at least inevitable;

we let our hems up, our guard down.

We believed you relic, symbolic, labeled

2016 the year of your resurrection;

we named you a nation, and ourselves

your ecstatic citizens. We pranced

our pantsuit joy. Perhaps, like some

of us, you always suspected this betrayal

—the quirky reenactment turned final battle,

the enemy returned hydra-headed, fanged,

and multitudinous, and you, sweet

suit, mere thread and dream against it.

Perhaps the two-pieced double consciousness

of you always knew you might not emerge

unbedraggled. Still, I salute you, pantsuit,

vow to dust the dirt from your war-worn seams,

pull you on, pull myself through: pantsuit up

and remember the truth we always knew—

you, pantsuit, are only as powerful

as the body that bears you.

LAUREN K. ALLEYNE

MADAME X—

she a hustler a hussy shaking her bustled booty
up and down town all smiles and wiles and whiffs
of possible//naughty naughty now you see her
whipping her hair waist corseted in shiny leather
now you see her buttoned to the throat flashing
a rogue ankle a sweet-boned wrist//now you see
her veiled all eyes and imagination and longing
heart strumming a set-me-free song just for you
for you// for you//maybe she will open her
mind her mouth her sweet-meat sumptin' sumptin'
maybe she'll let you touch-kiss-take everything
you can wrap your words around//starting here//
starting with her goddamn name

ANNE WALDMAN

MATRIOT ACTS

1.

~~+Patriot Act+~~
could drive a citizenry crazy

~~+Patriarch+~~
Adam to Noah, 12 tribes of Israel, progenitors of the human race

~~+Patriarchal?+~~
how far in Empire can you go descending through the father further?

~~+Paternalism+~~
noblesse oblige: laboratories, genocide of Native Americans
likely now as in China… Tibetans, Quighers

down the line: nostalgia for a lost thread

~~+Pater Familias+~~
political dynasties, endless rule…

~~+Patronomic+~~
sound the metronome

+Patronizing?+

arrogance, condescension

+Paternity?+

who birthed whom, what myth immigration "below the border"

+Pathology?+

dark light, dark site, the war machine, crimes against *humanitas*

+Pathological?+

it worsens…crimes against a woman's body

+Pathetic?+

caves in, you want to run and hide yourself from the special operatives world

+Pathogenic?+

white man privileged toxic ethos a fatwa

+Patricentric?+

ethos? centripetal

+Patrilinear?+

centrifugal

+Patrimonial?+

enough

+Patrist?+

let my sisters go

+Patron?+

    slave trade, oppression

+Padrone?+

    metabolic, corrupt

+Patronage?+

    lobbying etc

+Patriot?+

    seriously? are you serious?

+Patriot Act?+

    euphemism for torture, control, surveillance, eternal arms trade, and all crimes against women

Chorus: call "matriot" – "matriot" *is called*

        call "matriarchal" – *"matriarchal" called*

        call "matriarchy" – *"matriarchy" is called*

        call "matrilineal" – *"matrilinear" called*

        call "matricentered" – *to be considered*

        call "matricentric" – *jury's out*

        call "matriotism" – *the true patriots*

Chorus: matrist – yes

matriot acts

matriot acts

matriot acts

2.

Invoke the hyena in petticoats!
laughing hyena, spotted hyena, striped -
all stalk the charnel ground amidst
microscopic & telescopic worlds
a step ahead of what is to come in lineage
in gratitude, in naming *las madres*
in naming *las mujeres*, in naming
the demands of our bodies
look for reclamation, sniff it out…
in a voice not my own but all of them
the wizened ductile face of slumbering female memory:
beginning of time, the timepiece of time
she who was the mother of a ghost ship
Ship of Locked Awe and subjugated dream
she who could never be reduced to a "gender issue"
she who announced a talismanic bond to planet
who saw vole tracks in the snow once on a

radical poet's tiny death plot
(*touch us, touch us with crenellated beauty now*)
may plead particles in the sunlight, a democratic grace
who documented all hurts and slights & transmuted them
to poetry, to flesh,
she was a challenge in my heart, the penultimate mother
"Denial Silences Violence" "Remember the Suffragettes"
O mothers of the shaking tent ceremony
mothers of the bifurcated space
mother of what goes on in your head
mothers of restless night start up in dream to new poetry
shock the animalized spirit!
splice into the virtual movie: be kind
crone: an old mobility
subject: be kind and keep moving
object: planet, of kindness towards sweet redress
protect the children that is your genetic command
object: more resistance metabolism
mothers of dilation & expansion
mothers with field guides
mothers with centripetal force
mothers rumpled
mothers at the matrix
mothers with weapons hidden in their hair
a bayonet in a tattoo in the shape of a skull-at-arms
this was what we were up against

as young girls stood up for their dream in the way of life
the fair sex will retaliate
the dark sex will retaliate
a fair break, justice in love?
what takes it: to break a stupor
what takes: a new metabolic modus
what takes: an antithetical hallucination
new narrations, tensions, take back: *stoned for adultery*
all actions reversed in masculine time
horoscopes read & remarked upon
what is in my stars? what planets rule?
mythical anti-fascist space & be a mutable form, a shape-shifter
be that little girl with her tiny instruments
who investigates the female cosmos
be next to her as she works overtime in the scriptorium
brewing her witchy stew

IN SUPPORT OF VIOLENCE

Two hundred Indian women killed their rapist on the courtroom floor of Nagpur in 2004.
When Police tried to arrest lead perpetrators // the women responded "arrest us all."

•

In this windowless room // where he poured acid & stole money // arrest
us all
In this windowless room [shut like the gut of an ox] arrest us all

Gored & gorge are words to describe a wound   Gorgeous // the
opening
Of a blade inside his chest   Gorgeous // black galaxies, growing

Across his skin, we threw rocks & chili pepper
Arrest us all

On the railroad tracks // where he murdered our sisters & left their dead
bodies
On the railroad tracks // where black ants began // biting crowns into

Calves //   The world is spinning and we're // falling from
its bed
How could we mourn?   He kept killing // & threatening // & raping
us

Arrest us all   On the red puddle // on the white
    courthouse floor
Arrest us all   We sawed his penis off // & tore his house // to
    rubble

Look // the streets are swarming // in protests   [welcome
    home]
The night is neon & buzzing like bumblebees

We never wanted to kill // only to stay alive // &
We waited like virgins // for the gentleness of strangers // to help or
    empathize.

ACHY OBEJAS

THE MARCH

I am about to step outside, I am about to step outside to the elements and my anticipation is a long inhalation that covers the world upon release. This is the beginning of a movement based on facts and not on sentiment or pronouncements, though both sentiment and pronouncements are useful and worthy. As I begin to lift my left foot, my Sartorius muscle allows my knee to move up towards my body. I am joined by others, however they can join with me, others who have suffered, too, and are not afraid to continue suffering. What we seek is a new majority rooted in justice for all whose conscience is committed to ceasing wrongs and doing right. What we want is nothing about us without us. What we want is for each individual to define their own identity and expect that society will respect them. We shift our weight, unlock our knees. Arrange our bodies in the best way for each of us. For an instant, most of us are standing on one foot. We are not in a hurry. We are not dreaming. We are ready to give up everything, even our lives. We shall do it without violence because that is our conviction. What we want is freedom, what we want is the power to determine our destiny. As my left foot comes down, it is coordinated with my right and they match the equivalent movement of those who have joined me, and with whom I am joining. We are firmly rooted. Whenever possible, we let our limbs swing in a natural motion and keep our heads facing forward. What we want is the complete elimination of military forces, not just from this or that territory, but from every corner, every outpost, on earth. What we want is full and meaningful employment. What we want is decent, safe housing. What we want is an education that teaches us our true histories and their consequences on the present. As each of us lifts our right foot (or makes the equivalent movement to ambulate), we are now a perfectly synchronized force, even in our differences and occasional disorder. What we want is an immediate stop to state brutality and the assassination of black people, and native people, and disabled people, and trans people, and women, and children, and mothers and fathers who can only do so much because they are shackled by the very state that seeks to kill them for having foolishly believed they were free. What we want are the doors flung open to Folsom, Riker's, Guantanamo, San Quentin, San Juan de Lurigancho, ADX Florence Supermax, La Sabaneta, Attica, Camp 22, Pollsmoor. It would be fatal to overlook the urgency of the moment. As we advance, we are a thunderous thrum. Some of us will run under the rain in Seattle, and toward traffic to block Lake Shore Drive in Chicago. Others will flood Wall Street and more will storm the port of Oakland. There will be one lonely soul in snowy Bethel, Alaska, and clusters in Little Rock, in sweltering Ferguson, in Tallahassee and Flagstaff, Baltimore, Detroit, Honolulu, Boise, in ancient Salem, Wichita and Northampton, Oklahoma City and Spearfish, South Dakota. And always on the mall in Washington, always on the green, always in the bitter cold that is Pennsylvania Avenue. Nerve and muscle adapt to the rhythmic stimulus of our own noise, the noise we make together. It is

true that when in the course of human events, it becomes necessary for
one person to connect to another and another and another in order to
defend our equality, our difference, our dependence on one another, then

Author's Note: Text adapted from The Black Panthers Ten Point Program, The
Delano Manifesto, Equalise It! (a disability manifesto), Martin Luther King Jr.'s "I
Have a Dream" Speech, Trail of Broken Treaties, The Transfeminist Manifesto and
the Declaration of Independence of the United States of America.

MAUREEN MCLANE

MEANWHILE

The plum thong's
been abandoned so long
under the picnic table
I think it's fair to say
it's trash unless you're into
that kind of recycling.
The ganja's more open
now, not quite legal,
not quite not. I have a need
for relief, for calm,
for the buzz a woman's
voice lowly sounding itself
in the night air might bring.
*Are you here for the swim
or the scream?* I know
I'll get both there's no avoiding.
I am almost depressed
as a reflective climate scientist
and all the old apocalypses
seem peculiarly optimistic

though perhaps that's an optical
illusion of my 21st century eyes
which are as you can see
astigmatic. How do you work
and where? Will you leave Brooklyn
for Detroit? Do you think
America's blacks are fatally bound
to the horizon of nation?
America's whites?
They are having to know now
their whiteness
O Ho Yes They We Are
Meanwhile the ferns
are still green,
prehistoric, maybe posthistoric
if history's ceded everything
to geography, ecology, biology from here
on out. Meanwhile I might swim.
I might watch Von Trier's *Melancholia*
again and cheer up. I might decide
finally to move to the west coast
near Seattle, say, a town destined
to be destroyed very soon
if statistics about the fault are true.

MAUREEN MCLANE

HEIDENRÖSLEIN

sexual idyll
sustained by a pill

yr libido
his speedo

daterape drug
shot, mug

not she said
he said

none bled
none wed
none dead

ELLEN HAGAN

TO THE BREASTS WHEN IT'S OVER –

You two heave heavies, glory rockers
right-on drop gold rum bumpers.

Didn't you divine & dine, feed &
fortify – you heaven-ed helpers, plenty

planters, mystifiers mag-fucking-nificent
the fact you fed for five years & now.

You make me mourn & moan, make
merry w/ *it's over*. Sure the baby

still needing nighttime nursing, you
dwindle to dribble. Infant to toddler

god (damn) soon enough these girls
will be *those girls* as you watch them

walkrunjumpdanceplaypunksneakdive
away from you. But you won't forget

there was a time when all their hunger
was quenched. By you.

TO THE WOMAN ON ST. NICHOLAS AVENUE WHOSE THIGH WAS A WILDERNESS BLOOMING —

There you sat, gardenias & fat lemon trees bursting forth
from what appeared to be vulva – very near upper-most thigh.
That place we all of us blossom out from. You with all
your gnarled pinkest roses streaming upwards, all froth & funk
from the newspaper stand – none of it could contain
the many multitudes shooting forth from your thigh, how
it was full of satsumas & mangoes alike, sweet syrup of the streets.

All of you looked ragged & ravaged & I'm not one to judge, as much
of me looks the same so much of the time. & none of us immune to
tolls the days take & all of us whole reveling in the days given.
But my god – what contrast was your knee to your hip, what bright hot
youth. How a body part can so quickly become avocado tree, magnolia,
peony, the way one opens up like sex, the way a clitoris swells
& swolls, how deep & divine a leg can look all draped over workhorse
right there in the middle stench/steam of city living.

Look, I want to say, *look at this woman with her whole billowing self* (even as the rest of her is fading). All that ink on all that skin. God, what a garden of a woman. What catapult, what precision. All, all of her springing upwards & alive.

LUCKY LADIES SESTINA

for Josey, on her 50th birthday

I wake up with you, warm in the dark blankets, safe
our whole lives but still sort of surprised. Lucky ladies,
living together, up in our own damn house. No sick babies,
no hunger, getting yelled at, getting hit. We get to be alive now,
rescued by here, by us. Some equity, our plenty of time. Back then
my grandma's mom got given away, parents too poor

to keep her. My grandfather lived in a Masonic Home for Poor
Widows and Orphans, dropped off by his dad when an unsafe
abortion killed their mom. They never knew. Back then
button hooks, bleeding out in bathtubs: the family's ladies
knew all about it, but nobody told the men. Now
nobody dies. Here. Because of that. But plenty of babies

go unwanted, and whole families leave Syria, bring babies
we seem to think are proto-terrorists. Humans! Poor
humans, so sure we deserve everything we have now.
Plus more. Sure everything's earned, nothing sacrificed to be safe
as houses here. I like to think of the ships and tenements, loony
        bins, ladies
hating staying home but doing it, saddled with proto-us. And then

think of our problems: the oil bill, AAA, overdraft charges, UPS. Back
	then
we'd probably be whores, or witches, all our rape-babies
born to die young. We read about corpse meditation, meet ladies
for lunch in museums, choose new wines. I meditate on prison, the poor
prisoners, fluorescent quiver of those classrooms, their chill. Safe
to say I'm spoiled. A car! A dishwasher! A dryer! We hustled. Now
we hunker down. You know every decent bartender in town now;
most of them you trained your sweet self, your swole knees. Back then
I taught seven classes, you pulled shifts through pneumonia, only safe
with that money coming in. I teach *deeds* dancing in a *green bay*, bees
being *buccaneers of buzz*, make Sestina Worksheets for my poor
students: hungry grad students, undergrads working four jobs, ladies
on probation in the Southie Court House, cafeterias full of ladies
still in jail. Even they, alive today, can't understand me now,
how I was confused when a guard yelled at me, explained to the poor
ladies *Nobody tells me what to do*. They were stunned, said *Dag*, then
we got back to work. Their essays on Desdemona, Lady MacBeth's
	babies.
You and I decide what we want for dinner: someplace new or something
	safe,
a Caesar salad, roast chicken. Ladies love chicken, a glass of red wine.
	Then
we nestle down with our books, silken sleep. Now we sleep like babies,
safe as houses, for all those poor babies before us, who never got to be
	safe.

JENNY JOHNSON

FOLSOM STREET FAIRYTALE

Once upon a time her cheeks were Popsicle red and the leather a licorice
     twist.

Once upon a time she swung you like a cub by your scruff.

Once upon a time clamped nipples like twin satellites.

Once upon a time whatever she strapped on turned into a swan.

Bent over in studded chaps, she could be anyone:

The next door neighbor, a hockey mom, a public defender,

the bank teller with those long lashes.

JENNY JOHNSON

THERE ARE NEW WORLDS

To ride a horse is holy.
Like how Stephen refusing to ride side saddle
in *The Well of Loneliness*

fully astride, rides high on
the acrid sweat
of leather.

On the overleaf of my worn copy,
there by the pond, next to Stephen
isolated on a stone, is a swan.

I first kissed a woman
after hours of silence and shared cherry Chap Stick
late at night on a bench

in a garden that was so historical
Thomas Jefferson must have sat there, too
cross legged in his wig

or Gertrude Stein, I hope, legs straddled wide
on a speaking tour
explaining, *A rose is a rose is a rose*

I strode home alone
cutting through
the icy November chill

like a cygnet paddling
suddenly
in a fresh, dark lake.

CONTRIBUTORS

ELIZABETH ACEVEDO is the youngest child and only daughter of Dominican immigrants. She holds a BA in Performing Arts from the George Washington University and an MFA in Creative Writing from the University of Maryland. She is a National Poetry Slam Champion. *The Poet X* (HarperCollins, 2018) is her debut novel.

KIM ADDONIZIO is the author of seven poetry collections, two novels, two story collections, and two books on writing poetry, *The Poet's Companion* (with Dorianne Laux) and *Ordinary Genius*. She has received fellowships from the NEA and Guggenheim Foundation, two Pushcart Prizes, and was a National Book Award Finalist for her collection *Tell Me*. Her latest books are *Mortal Trash: Poems* (W. W. Norton) and a memoir, *Bukowski in a Sundress* (Penguin). She recently collaborated on a chapbook, *The Night Could Go in Either Direction* (Slapering Hol) with poet Brittany Perham. Addonizio also has two word/music CDs: *Swearing, Smoking, Drinking, & Kissing* (with Susan Browne) and *My Black Angel*, a companion to *My Black Angel: Blues Poems & Portraits*, featuring woodcuts by Charles D. Jones.

KAVEH AKBAR's poems appear recently in *The New Yorker*, *Poetry*, *The Nation*, and *The New York Times*. His first book, *Calling a Wolf a Wolf*, is just out with Alice James in the US and Penguin in the UK.

DANIEL ALBANESE is the New York City-based photographer and filmmaker behind the website TheDustyRebel. Shaped by his background in anthropology, he has built a worldwide following documenting the more marginal aspects of the urban landscape, as well as controversial artworks, political protests, and city living. He has lectured at several universities about his work, contributed to a number of street art books, and has appeared in multiple documentaries. In 2017, he began production on his first feature length documentary and book exploring the global Queer Street Art movement.

LAUREN K. ALLEYNE is the author of *Difficult Fruit* (Peepal Tree Press, 2014). She holds an MFA in Poetry and a graduate certificate in Feminist, Gender, and Sexuality Studies from Cornell University, and an MA in English and Creative Writing from Iowa State University. Alleyne's fiction, non-fiction, interviews, and poetry have been widely published in journals and anthologies such as *Women's Studies Quarterly*, *Guernica*, *The Caribbean Writer*, *Black Arts Quarterly*, *Crab Orchard Review*, *Gathering Ground*, and *Growing Up Girl*, among others. Her work has earned several honors and awards, most recently the Picador Guest Professorship in Literature at the University of Leipzig, Germany, a 2014 Iowa Arts Council Fellowship, and first place in the 2016 Split This Rock Poetry Contest. Alleyne is a Cave Canem graduate, and is originally from Trinidad and Tobago. She is currently assistant director of the Furious Flower Poetry Center and Associate Professor of English at James Madison University.

RYKA AOKI is the author of *Seasonal Velocities*, *He Mele a Hilo (A Hilo Song)*, and *Why Dust Shall Never Settle Upon This Soul*. She is a two-time Lambda Award finalist and the winner of a University Award from the Academy of American Poets. She has appeared in *Publishers Weekly*, the *Huffington Post*, and was honored by the California State Senate for "extraordinary commitment to the visibility and well-being of Transgender people." She is a professor of English at Santa Monica College. You can find her at rykaryka.com.

JUDITH BAUMEL is a poet, critic, and translator. She is a professor of English and founding director of the Creative Writing Program at Adelphi University. Her most recent book is *The Kangaroo Girl*.

SANDRA BEASLEY is the author of three poetry collections: *Count the Waves* (W. W. Norton, 2015); *I Was the Jukebox* (W. W. Norton, 2010), winner of the Barnard Women Poets Prize; and *Theories of Falling* (New Issues Poetry & Prose, 2008), winner of the New Issues Poetry Prize, as well as *Don't Kill the Birthday Girl: Tales from an Allergic Life*, a memoir. In 2015 she received a fellowship from the National Endowment for the Arts. She lives in Washington, DC, and is on the faculty of the low-residency MFA program at the University of Tampa.

ROSEBUD BEN-ONI Born to a Mexican mother and Jewish father, Rosebud Ben-Oni is a recipient of the 2014 NYFA Fellowship in Poetry and a CantoMundo Fellow. She is the author of *SOLECISM* (Virtual Artists Collective, 2013), a contributor to *The Conversant*, and an Editorial Advisor for VIDA: Women in Literary Arts. Her poems appear in *POETRY, The American Poetry Review, TriQuarterly, Prairie Schooner, Arts & Letters,* and *Hunger Mountain,* among others. Recently, her poem "Poet Wrestling with Angels in the Dark" was commissioned by the National September 11 Memorial & Museum in New York City. She writes weekly for *The Kenyon Review* blog, and teaches creative writing at UCLA Extension's Writers' Program. Find her at 7TrainLove.org.

JERICHO BROWN is the recipient of a Whiting Writers Award and of fellowships from the John Simon Guggenheim Foundation, the Radcliffe Institute for Advanced Study at Harvard University, and the National Endowment for the Arts. His poems have appeared in *The New York Times* and *The New Yorker*. His first book, *Please* (New Issues 2008), won the American Book Award. His second book, *The New Testament* (Copper Canyon 2014), won the Anisfield-Wolf Book Award. He is an associate professor of English and Creative Writing and the Director of the Creative Writing Program at Emory University in Atlanta.

MAHOGANY L. BROWNE The Cave Canem, Poets House, and Serenbe Focus alum is the author of several books including *Redbone* (nominated for NAACP Outstanding Literary Works), and *#Dear Twitter: Love Letters Hashed Out Online in 140 Characters or Less*, (recommended by Small Press Distribution and About.com Best Poetry Books of 2010). Mahogany bridges the gap between lyrical poets and literary emcee. She has toured Germany, Amsterdam, England, Canada, and recently Australia as one-third of the cultural arts exchange project Global Poetics. Her journalism has been published in the magazines *Uptown*, *KING*, *XXL*, *The Source*, Canada's *The Word* and the UK's *MOBO*. Her poetry has been published in literary journals *Pluck*, *Manhattanville Review*, *Muzzle*, *Union Station Mag*, *Literary Bohemian*, *Bestiary*, *Joint* and *The Feminist Wire*. She is the co-editor of the forthcoming anthology *The Break Beat Poets: Black Girl Magic* and the chapbook collection *Kissing Caskets* (Yes Yes Books). She is an Urban Word NYC Artistic Director (as seen on HBO's *Brave New Voices*), founder of Women Writers of Color Reading Room, Program Director of BLM@Pratt, and facilitates performance poetry and writing workshops throughout the country. Browne is also the publisher of Penmanship Books, the Nuyorican Poets Café Friday Night Slam curator, and a recent graduate of Pratt Institute's MFA Writing and Activism program.

DANIELLE CHAPMAN is the author of a collection of poems, *Delinquent Palaces*, published by Northwestern University Press in 2015. Her poems have been published in *The New Yorker*, *The Atlantic Monthly*, and *Poetry* magazine. "The Country Way," a group of essays about her family's 1790 farmhouse in Middle Tennessee, appears in the fall 2017 issue of the *Oxford American*.

LAUREN CLARK's first collection of poems, *Music for a Wedding*, was selected by Pulitzer Prize-winner Vijay Seshadri for the 2016 AWP Donald Hall Prize in Poetry. It was published by the University of Pittsburgh Press in 2017. They hold a BA in Classics from Oberlin College and an MFA in poetry from the University of Michigan, where they were the recipient of four Hopwood Awards. They collaborate with Etc. Gallery in Chicago.

KWAME DAWES is the author of twenty-one books of poetry and numerous other books of fiction, criticism, and essays. In 2016 his book *Speak from Here to There*, a co-written collection of verse with Australian poet John Kinsella, appeared along with *When the Rewards Can Be So Great: Essays on Writing and the Writing Life* (Pacific University Press) which he edited. His most recent collection, *City of Bones: A Testament* (Northwestern University Press), appeared in 2017. Also in 2017, Dawes co-edited with Matthew Shenoda, *Bearden's Odyssey: Poets Responding to the Art of*

Romare Bearden (Northwest University Press). His awards include the Forward Prize for Poetry, The Hollis Summers Poetry Prize, The Musgrave Silver Medal, several Pushcart Prizes, the Barnes and Nobles Writers for Writers Award, and an Emmy. He is Glenna Luschei Editor of *Prairie Schooner* and Chancellor Professor of English at the University of Nebraska. He also teaches in the Pacific MFA Program. Dawes serves as the Associate Poetry Editor for Peepal Tree Books and is Director of the African Poetry Book Fund. He is Series Editor of the African Poetry Book Series, and Artistic Director of the Calabash International Literary Festival.

SAFIA ELHILLO is the author of *The January Children* (University of Nebraska Press, 2017). Sudanese by way of Washington, DC, she received a BA from NYU's Gallatin School of Individualized Study and an MFA in poetry at the New School. Safia is a Pushcart Prize nominee, co-winner of the 2015 Brunel University African Poetry Prize, and winner of the 2016 Sillerman First Book Prize for African Poets. She has received fellowships from Cave Canem, The Conversation, and Crescendo Literary and The Poetry Foundation's Poetry Incubator. In addition to appearing in several journals and anthologies including *The BreakBeat Poets: New American Poetry in the Age of Hip-Hop*, her work has been translated into Arabic, Japanese, Estonian, and Greek. With Fatimah Asghar, she is co-editor of the anthology *Halal If You Hear Me*. She is currently a teaching artist with Split This Rock.

LAURA FAIRGRIEVE received her MFA from Adelphi University. She is a 2016 winner of the Poets & Writers Amy Award. Her work has appeared in *Mortar Magazine*, *Underwater New York*, *Inscape Magazine*, *The Bitchin' Kitsch*, *Ink in Thirds*, *East Coast Ink*, and *Words Dance Publishing*, among others. She lives in Brooklyn. To see her work visit laurafairgrieve.com.

DENICE FROHMAN is an award-winning poet, performer, and educator. She is a 2014 CantoMundo Fellow, 2013 Women of the World Poetry Slam Champion, and former Leeway Transformation Award recipient. Her work has appeared on ESPN, the *Huffington Post*, is forthcoming in *Nepantla: An Anthology for Queer Poets of Color*, and garnered over 7.5 million views online. She has featured at over 200 colleges and universities; hundreds of high schools, non-profits, and cultural arts spaces; and performed at The White House in 2016. She has a Master's in Education and works with The Philly Youth Poetry Movement. Currently, she tours the country.

ELLEN HAGAN is a writer, performer, and educator. Her poetry collections include: *Hemisphere*, published by Northwestern University Press in 2015, and *Crowned*, published by Sawyer House Press in 2010. Ellen's poems and essays can be found on ESPNW, in the pages of *Creative Nonfiction*, *Underwired Magazine*, *She Walks in Beauty*, and *Southern Sin*. Ellen's performance work has been showcased at The New York International Fringe and Los Angeles Women's Theater Festival. She is the recipient of the 2013 NoMAA Creative Arts Grant and received grants from the Kentucky Foundation for Women and the Kentucky Governor's School for the Arts. National arts residencies include The Hopscotch House and Louisiana Arts Works. She is the Director of Poetry and Theatre Programs at the DreamYard Project. Visit her online at www.ellenhagan.com or on Twitter @ellenhagan.

JAMES ALLEN HALL's first book of poetry, *Now You're the Enemy*, won awards from the Lambda Literary Foundation, the Texas Institute of Letters, and the Fellowship of Southern Writers. He is the recipient of fellowships from the National

Endowment of the Arts, the New York Foundation of the Arts, and the University of Arizona Poetry Center, as well as the Bread Loaf Writers' Conference and the Sewanee Writers' Conference. His second book, *I Liked You Better Before I Knew You So Well*, is a collection of personal lyric essays. The book was selected by author Chris Kraus as the winner of the Cleveland State University Poetry Center Press's Essay Award. He is Associate Professor of English at Washington College in Maryland and Director of the Rose O'Neill Literary House.

FRANCINE J. HARRIS is the author of *play dead*, winner of the 2017 Lambda Literary and Audre Lorde Awards, and a finalist for the 2017 Hurston/Wright Legacy Award. Her first collection, *allegiance*, was a finalist for the 2013 Kate Tufts Discovery and PEN Open Book Awards. Originally from Detroit, she has received a fellowship from the National Endowment for the Arts, is a Cave Canem poet, and is currently Writer in Residence at Washington University in St. Louis.

TYEHIMBA JESS is the author of two books of poetry, *Leadbelly* and *Olio*. *Olio* won the 2017 Pulitzer Prize, the Anisfield-Wolf Book Award, and The Midland Society Author's Award in Poetry, and received an Outstanding Contribution to Publishing Citation from the Black Caucus of the American Library Association. It was also nominated for the National Book Critics Circle Award, the PEN Jean Stein Book Award, and the Kingsley Tufts Poetry Award. *Leadbelly* was a winner of the 2004 National Poetry Series. *Library Journal* and *Black Issues Book Review* both named it one of the "Best Poetry Books of 2005." Jess, a Cave Canem and NYU Alumnus, received a 2004 Literature Fellowship from the National Endowment for the Arts, and was a 2004–05 Winter Fellow at the Provincetown Fine Arts Work Center. Jess is also a veteran of the 2000 and 2001 Green Mill Poetry Slam Team, and won a 2000–01 Illinois Arts Council Fellowship in Poetry, the 2001 *Chicago Sun-Times* Poetry Award, and a 2006 Whiting Fellowship. He presented his poetry at the 2011 TedX Nashville Conference and won a 2016 Lannan Literary Award in Poetry. Jess is a Professor of English at the College of Staten Island.

JENNY JOHNSON is the author of *In Full Velvet* (Sarabande Books, 2017). She is the recipient of a 2015 Whiting Award and a 2016-17 Hodder Fellowship in Poetry at Princeton University. Her poems have appeared in the *Los Angeles Review of Books Quarterly*, *New England Review*, *Troubling the Line: Trans and Genderqueer Poetry and Poetics*, and elsewhere. She teaches at the University of Pittsburgh and at the Rainier Writing Workshop, Pacific Lutheran University's low-residency MFA program.

KIMBERLY JOHNSON is the author of three collections of poetry, most recently *Uncommon Prayer* (Persea, 2014). With her spouse Jay Hopler, she edited *Before the Door of God: An Anthology of Devotional Poetry* (Yale University Press, 2013). She has also published poems in translation from Latin and Greek and a number of critical works on Renaissance literature. Recipient of grants and awards from the Guggenheim Foundation, the NEA, and the Utah Arts Council, she lives in Salt Lake City.

AMANDA JOHNSTON earned a Master of Fine Arts in Creative Writing from the University of Southern Maine. She is the author of two chapbooks, *GUAP* and *Lock & Key*, and the full-length collection *Another Way to Say Enter* (Argus House Press). Her poetry and interviews have appeared in numerous online and print publications, among them, *Callaloo*, *Poetry*, *Kinfolks*, *Quarterly*, *Muzzle*, *Pluck!*, and the anthologies *Small Batch*, *di-vêrsé-city*, and *The Ringing Ear: Black Poets Lean South*. The recipient of multiple Artist Enrichment grants from the Kentucky Foundation for

Women and the Christina Sergeyevna Award from the Austin International Poetry Festival, she is a member of the Affrilachian Poets and a Cave Canem graduate fellow. Johnston is a Stonecoast MFA faculty member, a cofounder of Black Poets Speak Out, and founding executive director of Torch Literary Arts.

JACQUELINE JONES LAMON is the author of two collections, *Last Seen*, a Felix Pollak Poetry Prize selection, and *Gravity, U.S.A.*, recipient of the Quercus Review Press Poetry Series Book Award; and the novel, *In the Arms of One Who Loves Me*. Noted by the NAACP in the category of Outstanding Literature, Poetry, LaMon is the recipient of honors for her commitment to university teaching, her social and literary criticism, and her creative work. LaMon is the immediate past president of Cave Canem Foundation, Inc., an organization committed to cultivating the artistic and professional growth of African American poets. She lives in New York and teaches at Adelphi University.

JADE LASCELLES is a poet, editor, and letterpress printer based in Boulder, Colorado. Her creative and critical work has been featured in the likes of *Gesture*, *Periodic*, *Something on Paper*, and the Ed Bowes film *Gold Hill*. She is the current editor-in-chief of *Bombay Gin Literary Journal* and a founding member of the publishing collective Precipice. In addition to a career in editing, she teaches courses on writing and small press publishing and manages the Harry Smith Print Shop at Naropa University. Her first book *Proximate Seams* and a co-edited anthology by Precipice are both forthcoming.

DOROTHEA LASKY is the author of five books of poetry, most recently the forthcoming *Milk* (Wave Books), as well as *ROME* (W.W. Norton/Liveright) and *Thun-*

derbird, Black Life, and *AWE*, all out from Wave Books. She is also the author of several chapbooks, including most recently *Snakes* (Tungsten Press) and *Poetry is Not a Project* (Ugly Duckling Presse). She is the co-editor of *Open the Door: How to Excite Young People About Poetry* (McSweeney's) and is in the process of co-writing a book on astrology and poetry for Penguin Random House. She lives in New York City, where she is an Assistant Professor of Poetry in Columbia University's School of the Arts and co-directs the Columbia Artist/Teachers program.

ADA LIMÓN is the author of four books of poetry, including *Bright Dead Things*, which was named a finalist for the 2015 National Book Award in Poetry, a finalist for the Kingsley Tufts Poetry Award, a finalist for the 2015 National Book Critics Circle Award, and one of the Top Ten Poetry Books of the Year by *The New York Times*. Her other books include *Lucky Wreck*, *This Big Fake World*, and *Sharks in the Rivers*. She serves on the faculty of Queens University of Charlotte Low Residency MFA program, and the 24Pearl Street online program for the Provincetown Fine Arts Work Center. She also works as a freelance writer splitting her time between Lexington, Kentucky and Sonoma, California.

JILL MCDONOUGH is the author of *Habeas Corpus* (Salt, 2008), *Oh, James!* (Seven Kitchens, 2012), *Where You Live* (Salt, 2012), and *Reaper* (Alice James, 2017). The recipient of three Pushcart prizes and fellowships from the Lannan Foundation, the National Endowment for the Arts, the Fine Arts Work Center, the New York Public Library, the Library of Congress, and Stanford's Stegner program, she taught incarcerated college students through Boston University's Prison Education Program for thirteen years. Her work has appeared in *Poetry*, *Slate*, *The Nation*, *The Threepenny Review*, and *Best American Poetry*. She teaches in the MFA program at

UMass-Boston and directs 24PearlStreet, the Fine Arts Work Center online. Her fifth poetry collection, *Here All Night*, is forthcoming from Alice James Books.

KARYNA MCGLYNN is the author of *Hothouse* (Sarabande Books, 2017), *I Have to Go Back to 1994 and Kill a Girl* (Sarabande Books, 2009), and several chapbooks including *The 9-Day Queen Gets Lost on Her Way to the Execution* (Willow Springs Editions, 2016). Karyna holds an MFA in Poetry from the University of Michigan, and earned her PhD in Literature and Creative Writing from the University of Houston where she served as Managing Editor for *Gulf Coast*. Her honors include the Verlaine Prize, the Kathryn A. Morton Prize, the Hopwood Award, and the Diane Middlebrook Fellowship in Poetry at the University of Wisconsin. Karyna is currently a Visiting Assistant Professor of Literature & Languages at Christian Brothers University in Memphis. Find her online at www.karynamcglynn.com.

RACHEL MCKIBBENS is a two-time New York Foundation for the Arts poetry fellow and author of *Pink Elephant*, *Into the Dark & Emptying Field* and *blud*. She founded The Pink Door Women's Writing Retreat, the only annual writing retreat exclusively for women of color, and co-curates the acclaimed literary series Poetry & Pie Night in upstate New York.

MAUREEN MCLANE is the author of five books of poetry, including most recently *Some Say* (FSG, 2017), as well as *My Poets*, a hybrid of memoir and criticism. Her book *This Blue* was a Finalist for the 2015 National Book Award in Poetry.

NAOMI SHIHAB NYE is a lifetime traveler and educator who has found poetry everywhere she goes. She is author or editor of more than thirty books including

Transfer, Fuel, Red Suitcase, Honeybee, 19 Varieties of Gazelle, and the forthcoming *Voices in the Air—Poems for Listeners*.

ACHY OBEJAS is the author of the recent collection of short stories *The Tower of the Antilles* as well as the critically acclaimed novels *Ruins* and *Days of Awe*. Her poetry chapbook, *This is What Happened in Our Other Life*, was both a critical favorite and a bestseller. As a translator, she has worked with Junot Díaz, Wendy Guerra, Rita Indiana, Adam Mansbach, and many others.

CYNTHIA DEWI OKA is the author of *Salvage: Poems* and *Nomad of Salt and Hard Water*. A two-time Pushcart Prize Nominee, her poetry has appeared widely online and in print. She has been awarded the *Fifth Wednesday Journal* Editor's Prize in Poetry, and scholarships from the Voices of Our Nations (VONA) and Vermont Studio Center. As a 2016 Leeway Foundation Art and Change Grantee, she partnered with Asian Arts Initiative to create Sanctuary: A Migrant Poetry Workshop for immigrant poets in Philadelphia. She has also served as a poet mentor for *The Blueshift Journal*'s Speakeasy Project. Originally born and raised in Bali, Indonesia, Cynthia is currently based in Philadelphia, where she works as a Community Organizer with the New Sanctuary Movement, an interfaith immigrant justice organization. She is an MFA candidate at Warren Wilson College.

JOYCE PESEROFF's fifth book of poems, *Know Thyself*, was designated a "must read" by the 2016 Massachusetts Book Award. She is the editor of *The Ploughshares Poetry Reader, Robert Bly: When Sleepers Awake*, and *Simply Lasting: Writers on Jane Kenyon*. Her recent poems and reviews appear in *Consequence, Ibbetson Street, Memorious, New Ohio Review, Plume*, and on the website *The Woven Tale Press*. She directed

UMass Boston's MFA Program in its first four years, and currently blogs on writing and literature at joycepeseroff.com.

MARY RUEFLE is the author of *My Private Property* (Wave Books, 2016), *Trances of the Blast* (Wave Books, 2013), *Madness, Rack, and Honey: Collected Lectures* (Wave Books, 2012), a finalist for the National Book Critics Circle Award in Criticism, and *Selected Poems* (Wave Books, 2010), winner of the William Carlos Williams Award from the Poetry Society of America. She has published ten books of poetry, a book of prose (*The Most of It*, Wave Books, 2008), and a comic book, *Go Home and Go to Bed!* (Pilot Books/Orange Table Comics, 2007); she is also an erasure artist, whose treatments of nineteenth century texts have been exhibited in museums and galleries, and published in *A Little White Shadow* (Wave Books, 2006). Ruefle is the recipient of numerous honors, including the Robert Creeley Award, an Award in Literature from the American Academy of Arts and Letters, a Guggenheim fellowship, a National Endowment for the Arts fellowship, and a Whiting Award. She lives in Bennington, Vermont.

TRISH SALAH is the author of the Lambda Award-winning poetry collection *Wanting in Arabic*, and of *Lyric Sexology, Vol. 1*, as well as co-editor of a special issue of *TSQ* on Transgender Cultural Production. She is currently assistant professor of Gender Studies at Queen's University.

RUTH IRUPÉ SANABRIA's first collection of poetry, *The Strange House Testifies* (Bilingual Press), won 2nd place (Poetry) in the 2010 Annual Latino Book Awards. Her second collection of poems, *Beasts Behave in Foreign Land*, received the 2014

Letras Latinas/ Red Hen Press Award and was published in 2017. Her poems have appeared in anthologies such as *Women Writing Resistance* and *U.S. Latino Literature Today*. She works as a high school English teacher and lives with her husband and three children in Perth Amboy, New Jersey.

PATRICIA SMITH is the author of eight books of poetry, including *Incendiary Art; Shoulda Been Jimi Savannah*, winner of the Lenore Marshall Prize from the Academy of American Poets; *Blood Dazzler*, a National Book Award finalist; and *Gotta Go, Gotta Flow*, a collaboration with award-winning Chicago photographer Michael Abramson. Her other books include the poetry volumes *Teahouse of the Almighty, Close to Death, Big Towns Big Talk, Life According to Motown*; the children's book *Janna and the Kings* and the history *Africans in America*, a companion book to the award-winning PBS series. Her work has appeared in *Poetry, The Paris Review, The Baffler, The Washington Post, The New York Times, Tin House*, and in *Best American Poetry* and *Best American Essays*. She co-edited *The Golden Shovel Anthology—New Poems Honoring Gwendolyn Brooks* and edited the crime fiction anthology *Staten Island Noir*. Her contribution to that anthology won the Robert L. Fish Award from the Mystery Writers of America for the best debut story of the year and was featured in the anthology *Best American Mystery Stories*.

CHRISTOPHER SOTO aka Loma (b. 1991, Los Angeles) is a poet based in Brooklyn, New York. He is the author of *Sad Girl Poems* (Sibling Rivalry Press, 2016) and the editor of *Nepantla: A Journal Dedicated to Queer Poets of Color* (Nightboat Books, 2018). He cofounded the Undocupoets Campaign and worked with Amazon Literary Partnerships to establish grants for undocumented writers. In 2017, he was awarded "The Freedom Plow Award for Poetry & Activism" by Split This Rock and he was invited to teach a "Poetry and Protest Movements" course at Columbia University as part of the June Jordan Teaching Corp. In 2016, Poets & Writers honored him with the "Barnes & Noble Writer for Writers Award." He frequently writes book reviews for the Lambda Literary Foundation. His poems, reviews, interviews, and articles can be found at *The Nation*, *The Guardian*, *The Advocate*, *Los Angeles Review of Books*, *American Poetry Review*, *Tin House*, and more. His work has been translated into Spanish and Portuguese. He has been invited to speak at university campuses across the country. He is currently working on a full-length poetry manuscript about police violence and mass incarceration. He received his MFA in poetry from NYU, where he was a Goldwater Hospital Writing Workshop Fellow.

LAURA THEOBALD grew up in the Florida Keys and has lived in various places in the South. Her first full-length book of poetry is *What My Hair Says About You* from the Montreal-based small press publisher Metatron (2016). Her chapbooks are *Edna Poems* (Lame House, 2016), *The Best Thing Ever* (Boost House, 2015), and *Eraser Poems* (H_NGM_N, 2014). She completed her MFA in Poetry from LSU in 2016, and has served as an editor and book designer for a number of small press publishers. She is currently a book designer for BOAAT and OOMPH!, and a freelance editor and book designer. Her recent poems have appeared in *The Wanderer*, *Sink*, *Hobart*, *Pinwheel*, *Witch Craft Magazine*, *The Atlas Review*, *Everyday Genius*, *Black Warrior Review*, and other places. @lidleida / lauratheobald.tumblr.com.

ANASTACIA-RENEE is Civic Poet of Seattle and former 2015-17 Poet-in-Residence at Hugo House. She is a hybrid genre writer, workshop facilitator, and multivalent performance artist. She is the author of four books: *Forget It* (Black Radish Books), *(v.)* (Gramma Press), *Answer(Me)* (Argus Press), and *26* (Dancing Girl Press) and her poetry, prose and fiction have been published widely.

HOPE WABUKE is the author of *The Leaving* and *Movement No.1: Trains*. She is an Assistant Professor of English at the University of Nebraska-Lincoln and a contributing editor for *The Root*. Her work has been published in *Guernica*, *The Guardian*, *The North American Review*, *Ms. Magazine* online, and others. Hope has received fellowships and awards from the National Endowment for the Arts, Junot Diaz's Voices of Our Nations Arts Foundation, *The New York Times* Foundation, the Awesome Foundation, and the Barbara Deming Memorial Fund for Women Writers.

STACEY WAITE is Associate Professor of English at the University of Nebraska—Lincoln and has published four collections of poems: *Choke*, *Love Poem to Androgyny*, *the lake has no saint*, and *Butch Geography*. Waite's poems have appeared most recently in *Pittsburgh Poetry Review*, *Cherry Tree*, and *Court Green*. Waite's newest book is a mixed genre text entitled *Teaching Queer: Radical Possibilities for Writing and Knowing*, published by University of Pittsburgh Press.

ANNE WALDMAN has been a prolific and active poet and performer of her work for many years, creating radical new hybrid forms for the long poem, both serial and narrative, as with *Marriage: A Sentence*, *Structure of the World Compared to a Bubble*, and *Manatee/Humanity*, and most recently *Gossamurmur*. She is also the author of the magnum opus *The Iovis Trilogy: Colors in the Mechanism of Concealment*, a feminist "cultural intervention" which won the PEN Center 2012 Award for Poetry. She was awarded the American Book Award from the Before Columbus Foundation for Lifetime Achievement, 2015. She is the editor of *The Beat Book* and co-editor of *Civil Disobediences: Poetics and Politics in Action*, and *Beats At Naropa* and most recently *Cross Worlds: Transcultural Poetics. Voice's Daughter of a Heart Yet To Be Born* (Coffee House Press, 2016) continues her hybrid investigations. She is the recipient of the Shelley Memorial Award from the Poetry Society of America and a Chancellor of the Academy of American Poets.

ELIZABETH CLARK WESSEL is the author of four chapbooks, most recently *First one thing, and then the other* (forthcoming from Per Diem Press), and the translator of numerous Swedish novels, including *What We Owe* by Golnaz Hashemzadeh Bonde. She is also a founding editor at Argos Books. These days she calls Stockholm, Sweden home.

WENDY XU is most recently the author of *Phrasis* (Fence Books, 2017). The recipient of a Ruth Lilly Fellowship from the Poetry Foundation, her work has appeared in *The Best American Poetry, Boston Review, Poetry, A Public Space, BOMB*, and widely elsewhere. Born in Shandong, China in 1987, she lives in Brooklyn and is Poetry Editor for *Hyperallergic*.

MONIKA ZOBEL is the author of two books of poems—*An Instrument for Leaving*, selected by Dorothea Lasky for the 2013 Slope Editions Book Prize (Slope Editions, 2014), and *Das Innenfutter der Wörter* (edition keiper, Graz, Austria, 2015). Her poems and translations have appeared or are forthcoming in *Nimrod International Journal, Poetry Northwest, RHINO Poetry, Four Way Review, Redivider, DIAGRAM, Beloit Poetry Journal, Drunken Boat, Guernica Magazine, West Branch, Best*

New Poets 2010, and elsewhere. A Fulbright alumna and a Senior Editor at *The California Journal of Poetics*, Zobel divides her time between the US and Germany.

RACHEL ZUCKER is the author of nine books, most recently *The Pedestrians*. She teaches at NYU and is the host of Commonplace: Conversations with Poets (and Other People).

THE EDITORS

DANIELLE BARNHART is co-founding Editor & Director of Events for Village of Crickets. She coordinates programming for Adelphi University's MFA Program in Creative Writing, and teaches undergraduate creative writing part time. Winner of the 2015 Donald Everett Axinn Award in Poetry, she lives (and writes) on Long Island with her family.

IRIS MAHAN is a freelance writer, editor, and poet based in New York. She is a graduate of the University of Tennessee in Chattanooga and Adelphi University, where she was the recipient of the Robert Muroff Scholarship in Creative Writing, and co-founder of Village of Crickets. She works in nonprofit fundraising for the literary arts, most recently at PEN America and The Center for Fiction.

PERMISSIONS